DIG DEEPER INTO
1 & 2 KINGS

Andrew is co-pastor of Grace Church, Greenwich, and a tutor on the Cornhill training course. He lives at zero longitude with a big coffee machine with which he attempts to pour nice shapes into his coffee with steamed milk, and with Gustave, a hyperactive cocker spaniel. He (Gustave?) is a regular conference speaker and has co-written the *Dig Deeper* series, *Pierced for our Transgressions* and, most recently, *Are you 100% Sure You Want to Be an Agnostic?* He co-hosts Grace Pod, an expository podcast.

Alasdair is a lay elder at Crossway Stratford. He and Andrew first dug deeper into the Bible together in 2008 when Alasdair arrived in London to train as a barrister. In addition to arguing about law for a living, Alasdair enjoys (endures?) a household full of hair, shoes, good food and parties, and likes escaping to the great outdoors. He's co-written a couple of other books about inquests and environmental law, but you'll hopefully find this one more fun and spiritually rewarding.

'While there are many fine commentaries on every book of the Bible, most of these are written for students, scholars and pastors. Surprisingly, few commentaries are written for ordinary Christians. That's why I am happy to commend this volume on 1 & 2 Kings. The content is clear and accessible, and focused on the concerns and questions that thoughtful Christians often have. No doubt men and women of all ages in our churches will benefit from this careful exposition and from the others like it in this series.'
Kevin DeYoung, Senior Pastor of Christ Covenant Church, Matthews, North Carolina, and Associate Professor of Systematic Theology, Reformed Theological Seminary, Charlotte, North Carolina

'This book is a wonderful resource for those of us who want to know more about these pivotal books in the Old Testament. The authors write of "unearthing Bible treasure", and that is precisely what Andrew and Alasdair do as they carefully and forensically unpack 1 & 2 Kings for us. We are invited to study deeply, to join the authors in a growing understanding of God's sovereignty and his purposes. At the same time, this book is a serious, reverential and detailed exploration of Scripture, and also highly readable, at times even funny. I fully recommend it!'
Tim Farron, MP and author of *A Mucky Business*

'Good kings. Bad kings. Elijah and Elisha. Divided kingdom. Exile. These are the stories that make up 1 & 2 Kings, which can be fascinating to read but rather difficult to understand, interpret and apply. In *Dig Deeper into 1 & 2 Kings*, Andrew Sach and Alasdair Henderson present these stories with good humour and clarity, while also drawing out profound truths and making stunning connections to the whole of the Bible's story. This book will be my number-one recommendation for individuals or groups wanting to study these important books of the Bible.'
Nancy Guthrie, author of the Bible study series, *Seeing Jesus in the Old Testament*

'This book is not just "another Old Testament commentary". Trust me! The sermons I heard Andrew Sach preach on 1 & 2 Kings whetted my appetite for this book – and I have not been disappointed. Here is a commentary that not only makes you appreciate the Old Testament as it was intended to be understood by the original recipients, but also shows its abiding relevance with many light-bulb moments that leave you eager to preach 1 & 2 Kings as God's message to Christ's Church today.'
Conrad Mbewe, pastor of Kabwata Baptist Church and founding Chancellor of the African Christian University, Lusaka, Zambia

'This is another gem in the excellent *Dig Deeper* series. Seriousness about and close attention to the text of 1 & 2 Kings encourage and enable a richer understanding of these books. The authors help the reader of 1 & 2 Kings to work hard and to appreciate the unfolding story of God's wider purposes in the world. They allow God's revelation in these books to amplify our understanding of God's grace, salvation and judgement in the work of Christ. This book and this series are a great resource for churches.'
William Taylor, Rector of St Helen's Bishopsgate

'Many thoughtful Bible readers long for help and guidance in reading the Bible *more* thoughtfully. *Dig Deeper into 1 & 2 Kings* is a helpful, clear and practical guide to doing just that. The authors show-by-doing how asking pertinent questions (here called "tools") of the text under consideration enables the reader to pay closer attention to meaningful aspects of that text. Bible readers from beginners to old hands will be helped to "dig deeper", and so to discover more of the riches of God's wonderful word.'
John Woodhouse, former Principal, Moore Theological College, Sydney, and author of *1 Kings: Power, Politics and the Hope of the World*

DIG DEEPER INTO
1 & 2 KINGS

Andrew Sach and Alasdair Henderson

INTER-VARSITY PRESS
SPCK Group, Studio 101, The Record Hall, 16–16A Baldwin's Gardens, London
EC1N 7RJ, England
Email: ivp@ivpbooks.com
Website: www.ivpbooks.com

© Andrew Sach and Alasdair Henderson, 2025

Andrew Sach and Alasdair Henderson have asserted their rights under the Copyright, Designs and Patents Act 1988 to be identified as Authors of this work.

All rights reserved. No part of this publication may be reproduced, stored in a retrieval system, or transmitted, in any form or by any means, electronic, mechanical, photocopying, recording or otherwise, without the prior permission of the publisher or the Copyright Licensing Agency.

Scripture and other copyright acknowledgements can be found on page 216.

First published 2025

British Library Cataloguing-in-Publication Data
A catalogue record for this book is available from the British Library.

ISBN: 978–1–78974–516–0
eBook ISBN: 978–1–78974–517–7

Set in 11 on 14pt Minion Pro
Typeset in Great Britain by Fakenham Prepress Solutions, Fakenham, Norfolk
NR21 8NL
Printed in Great Britain by Ashford Colour Press Ltd, Gosport, Hampshire

Produced on paper from sustainable sources

Inter-Varsity Press publishes Christian books that are true to the Bible and that communicate the gospel, develop discipleship and strengthen the church for its mission in the world.

IVP originated within the Inter-Varsity Fellowship, now the Universities and Colleges Christian Fellowship, a student movement connecting Christian Unions in universities and colleges throughout Great Britain, and a member movement of the International Fellowship of Evangelical Students. Website: www.uccf.org.uk. That historic association is maintained, and all senior IVP staff and committee members subscribe to the UCCF Basis of Faith.

To the church family at Grace Church Greenwich,
and in particular to Hezekiah and Josiah,
born and named during a preaching series on 1 – 2 Kings;

and to the church family at Crossway Stratford and St Matthew's West Ham, as well as the members of the youth group at Bearsden Baptist Church 1997–2003, for fun, fellowship and first getting Alasdair to ask good questions about the Bible.

The Lord reigns; he is robed in majesty;
    the Lord is robed; he has put on strength as his belt.
Yes, the world is established; it shall never be moved.
Your throne is established from of old;
    you are from everlasting.

The floods have lifted up, O Lord,
    the floods have lifted up their voice;
    the floods lift up their roaring.
Mightier than the thunders of many waters,
    mightier than the waves of the sea,
    the Lord on high is mighty!

Your decrees are very trustworthy;
    holiness befits your house,
        O Lord, for evermore.
(Psalm 93)

The Lord has established his throne in the heavens,
    and his kingdom rules over all.
(Psalm 103:19)

The Bible toolkit

Here is a summary of the tools introduced in the first *Dig Deeper* book.[1]

AUTHOR'S PURPOSE TOOL
The biggest question we can ever ask of a passage in the Bible is simply, 'Why did the author write this?'

CONTEXT TOOL
Words come within sentences, sentences in paragraphs, paragraphs in chapters, chapters in sections ... If you take a text out of context you're left with a con!

STRUCTURE TOOL
How has the author broken down his material into sections? How do these sections fit together?

LINKING WORDS TOOL
Whenever you see a 'therefore', ask what it's there for! And the same goes for words like 'because', 'so that', 'for', etc.

PARALLELS TOOL
Bible poetry doesn't tend to rhyme. Instead, it says the same thing twice in different words (and so you get two chances at understanding it): 'Twinkle, twinkle little star; Shiny, shiny, tiny nebular.'

NARRATOR'S COMMENT TOOL
Sometimes the author breaks into his narrative to explain what's going on (a kind of 'Pssst, reader, make sure you understand this ...').

VOCABULARY TOOL
Bible words have Bible meanings. Be alert in case the

---

[1] Nigel Beynon and Andrew Sach, *Dig Deeper: Tools to unearth the Bible's treasure* (London: IVP, 2005).

author is using a familiar word in an unusual way.

TRANSLATIONS TOOL
Read the passage in more than one translation just in case there is a nuance one version has missed.

TONE AND FEEL TOOL
Pay attention to how the point is being made. Is it happy? Tragic? Comforting? Frightening? How does the author want you to feel about what he is saying?

REPETITION TOOL
Sometimes the author says something more than once to make sure we don't miss it. Sometimes the author says something more than once to make sure we don't miss it.

QUOTATION/ALLUSION TOOL
When the author quotes or alludes to another part of the Bible, we should turn there to see what ideas he is picking up on.

GENRE TOOL
There are many genres in the Bible – e.g., song, historical narrative, genealogy, law. Identifying the genre is important to how we interpret a passage.

COPYCAT TOOL
Is the author holding up one of his characters as someone we should imitate or whose likeness we should avoid?

BIBLE TIMELINE TOOL
Where is this passage on the Bible timeline? Where am I on the Bible timeline? How do I read this in the light of what has happened in between (e.g., the other side of Jesus)?

'WHO AM I?' TOOL
Whose shoes in the passage are we supposed to step into? If any!

'SO WHAT?!' TOOL
What implications does this have for me? For my church? For a non-Christian?

Introduction

'Blessed are the poor in spirit,' said Jesus, 'for theirs is the kingdom of heaven.' But this isn't a book about the Beatitudes. Jesus taught us to pray, 'Thy kingdom come.' But this isn't an exposition of the Lord's Prayer. The kingdom of God is arguably the most important theme in Jesus' teaching, but we can't understand it properly without going further back in time and immersing ourselves in the Old Testament books of (Samuel and) Kings. That's where the kingdom of God was first glimpsed on earth. That's where God shows us what good kings and bad kings look like. That's where we start to be dissatisfied with earthly rulers and to long for a heavenly one. That's what this book is about.

You probably know more of 1 – 2 Kings than you think. It's here that we read of the Temple being built, the 'still small voice' and the fall of Israel and Judah. It's where we meet wise Solomon, evil Jezebel and leprous Naaman. It's where we hear of the swashbuckling exploits of the prophets Elijah and Elisha, who between them do more miracles than anyone else in the Bible apart from Jesus. It has inspired famous music, from the 'Arrival of the Queen of Sheba' (which has accompanied many a bride down the aisle) to 'Zadok the Priest' (which has been played at every British coronation since George II) to 'Swing Low, Sweet Chariot' (a beautiful African–American spiritual which, for fascinating reasons, has become the theme tune of English rugby).[1] It offers enough material for a decade of Hollywood blockbusters, though please not from the studios that brought us *Noah* (the eco-warrior who wanted to kill his grandson) or *Exodus: Gods and Kings* (which

---

1 Caroline Lowbridge, 'Why is Swing Low, Sweet Chariot the England rugby song?' BBC News: www.bbc.co.uk/news/uk-england-51646140 (accessed 26 July 2024).

includes a plague of crocodiles and has God show up at the burning bush in the guise of a petulant child).[2] Who knows why filmmakers feel the need to tamper with the biblical screenplay, when the unedited original leaves even the best superhero franchise in the dust?

A big conviction driving every one of the *Dig Deeper* books is that there's more to be discovered in the Bible, if you look carefully. And by 'carefully', don't even think for a moment that you'll spot everything on first reading, or even second or third reading. Take care not to isolate yourself. Sometimes we need a little help from our friends, and when faced with a particularly tricky passage, we want to cry out, 'Help!' We need somebody who cares enough to dig deeper with us. That's the big conviction that drives us.

On initial reading, for example, you probably didn't notice that the first two sentences of the previous paragraph were acrostic: the first five words began with successive letters of the alphabet ('A b-ig c-onviction d-riving e-very …'). You may have missed the bookends, whereby the paragraph is topped and tailed with reference to a 'big conviction'. And did you spot the two allusions to songs by The Beatles? Or the fourfold repetition of the words 'care' or 'carefully'?

Admittedly, it was a clunky paragraph. Our attempt to include even a few of the literary devices routinely deployed by biblical authors was hard work, and it's given us a new respect for them, particularly given that their use of repetition, bookends or allusions is actually *purposeful*. We used The Beatles lyrics just for the fun of it, but when we notice that 1 Kings 12:28 echoes Exodus 32:4, it makes Jeroboam's sin a hundred times worse. We bookended a paragraph for no better reason than to show you that we could bookend a paragraph; the author of 1 – 2 Kings bookends the story of the Temple being built with two descriptions of Solomon's God-given wealth and wisdom, to show us that the whole project was of God from start to finish. Our repetition of 'carefully' was

---

2 *Noah*, directed by Darren Aronofsky (2014); *Exodus: Gods and Kings*, directed by Ridley Scott (2014).

Introduction

ham-fisted, but 2 Kings 11 repeats 'house' with a subtle wordplay that reveals how God is keeping one of the most important promises he ever made.

As with the other books in the *Dig Deeper* series, we are going to use some 'tools' to unearth some of these treasures. You can find a summary of the toolkit at the start of the book. But please don't think that understanding the Bible is a handle-turning mechanical process. We need to come to Scripture in sober recognition that this is our Creator speaking to us, willing to shape our lives in response to his voice:

> this is the one to whom I will look:
> > he who is humble and contrite in spirit
> > and trembles at my word.
>
> (Isaiah 66:2)

Like cooking a succulent pork belly, the other essential ingredient for good Bible study is time. If you flash-fry it on the hob, the verses will seem tough and chewy, and hard on the spiritual digestion. It must be slow roasted for hours. There's no substitute for growing familiar with the biblical text. The better you know it, the better you will discover you understand it.

One way of achieving this might be a three-hour Bible study, but that would be hard going. Instead, why not try to spend three hours on the same passage, but spread out over a week or two? Over many years our own churches have learned to build the slow-roast method into the way they do small groups, and it's been so foundational for our own Christian growth that we thought we'd share the concept with you:

Groups of between five and ten people study the same book of the Bible week by week. The leaders of these groups meet weekly or fortnightly in advance for a Study Leaders' Own Bible Study, more commonly referred to by its unflattering acronym. That means all leaders look at each passage twice. Except that we also ask the leaders to prepare at home for the SLOBS, and we ask everyone in the church to prepare at home for the main study. In addition, at the start of the year we have a leaders' training day to introduce the whole Bible book, and three or four times during the year we have a review evening, when we draw together the threads of what we've learned. At my (Andrew's) church we have even recently launched a podcast, 'Grace Pod', where we chat through the passage we looked at that week, so church members can keep mulling it over while they do their ironing/morning commute/gym session. The upshot of all this is that every leader looks at a passage seven times (training day, preparation, SLOBS, preparation, main study, review, podcast) and everyone else looks at it four times. By the end of all this, the biblical meat is succulent, and the crackling is to die for!

A slow-roast approach to *Dig Deeper into 1 & 2 Kings* might look like this. Start by reading the whole of 1 - 2 Kings over a couple of weeks (or listening to the superb David Suchet audio book, aka 'the Poirot Bible'[3]). Next, read again the particular section of 1 - 2 Kings you're about to tackle, and then read what we've written about it. Next, find a Christian friend with whom to share something you've learned. That will be one, two, three, four times. Not bad.

The motto of the *Dig Deeper* books is 2 Timothy 2:15: 'Do your best to present yourself to God as one approved, a worker who has no need to be ashamed, rightly handling the word of truth.' We've been praying that for ourselves each week as we sit down to write this. And we pray the same for you.

Getting our bearings

Even though this is a book about 1 - 2 Kings, it's important that we locate it within the story of the whole Bible, so don't be surprised if our journey from 1 Kings 1:1 to 2 Kings 25:30 includes detours from Abel to Zechariah.[4]

---

3 Available via Bible Gateway: www.biblegateway.com/audio/suchet/nivuk/1Kgs.1 (accessed 26 July 2024).

4 Sadly, the concept of an 'A to Z' only works in the Roman alphabet, so it's very unlikely to have been in Jesus' mind when he referred to 'Abel ... to Zechariah' in Matthew 23:35. Z is the sixth letter of the Greek alphabet and in the Hebrew alphabet it comes seventh. Oh well.

Introduction

If you had only three sentences to summarise the story of the whole Bible, what would you say? Here's our attempt:

- God made a good world.
- We stuffed it up.
- Jesus' death and resurrection fixes everything.

Notice this isn't just three facts, but three *events* that take place one after the other: it's a story. We've drawn it on a simple timeline below, which has evolved a bit since the first *Dig Deeper* book[5] (we are still learning!) so that it now ends higher on the right than it started on the left. In various ways, the Bible shows us that the world to come, having been redeemed by Jesus, is even better than the world as it was first created (see Figure 1).

Figure 1 **A brief history of time**

Within the story of humanity sits the story of Israel. Twelve chapters into the book of Genesis, God chooses a man called Abraham, and promises him that his descendants would be God's people, living in the promised land. It's later referred to as a 'land flowing with milk and honey' (Exodus 3:8), which didn't impress the teenagers on my (Andrew's) summer camp until I explained that these are essentially the ingredients that, boiled together, create the sauce in a sticky toffee pudding. In *Dig Deeper into*

---

[5] Beynon and Sach, *Dig Deeper*.

Exodus,[6] we explored the dramatic account of how the Israelites were rescued from slavery in Egypt and started on their way to possessing that land.

In *Dig Deeper into 1 & 2 Kings*, we shall read how, because of their persistent disobedience, the land 'vomited' them out (as Leviticus 18:28 puts it): a colourful metaphor that for parents of small children may also have associations with sticky toffee pudding! The exile happens in two stages, with the ten northern tribes (known as 'Israel') taken captive by the Assyrians in 722 BC, and the two southern tribes ('Judah') falling to the Babylonians in 586/7 BC. Meanwhile God sends prophets to announce a second great rescue that would see them returned to paradise. Isaiah describes this glorious future as 'new heavens and a new earth' (Isaiah 65:17). Ezekiel depicts it as a new Jerusalem where God dwells with his people, a city called 'The LORD Is There' (Ezekiel 48:35) (see Figure 2).

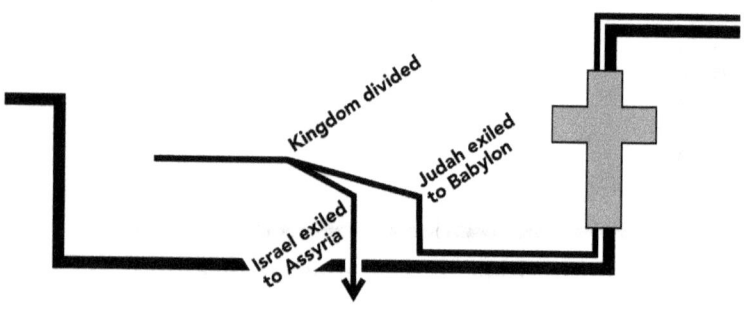

Figure 2 **The Israel story**

As we look at the two stories overlaid one on the other, it becomes obvious that one is a Russian-doll miniature of the other (see Table 1).

Notice that the stories converge: Jesus is both the last Adam and the new Israel. The hope of the godly Old Testament Jew is now the hope of every member of God's Church, whether Jew or Gentile.

---

6 Formerly published as Andrew Sach and Richard Alldritt, *Dig Even Deeper: Unearthing Old Testament treasure* (London: IVP, 2011).

Adam lived in	Israel lived in
the garden of Eden	the land of sticky toffee pudding
with a command from God (Genesis 2:17)	with God's law (Exodus 20)
which he broke	which they broke
and so was evicted	and so were exiled
until a Saviour came	until a Saviour came
(whom the Bible describes as the 'last Adam', 1 Corinthians 15:45)	(whom the Bible describes as a new 'Israel', e.g., Isaiah 49:3, 5-6)
to bring about a new heaven and new earth	to bring a new heaven and a new earth

Table 1 **History repeats itself**

There is another way of reading the Bible that tries to keep the two stories separate. According to that view, prophecies made to Israel are confined to ethnic Israel: the Jews lived in a land to the east of the Mediterranean and will do so again. They had a physical temple, which got destroyed, but they will have a physical temple again. Meanwhile, the Church is part of a different story or 'dispensation' which runs on a kind of parallel track.

Although many godly Christians have viewed things that way, it's not the way the apostles read the Old Testament. For example, 'Jerusalem' refers now to a heavenly city, not an earthly one (Galatians 4:25-31; Hebrews 11:10, 16; Revelation 21:1-2). The description of Israel as 'a kingdom of priests and a holy nation' is now applied directly to the Church (compare Exodus 19:6 with 1 Peter 2:9). The new temple is built not with stones but with Christians of diverse ethnicities (Ephesians 2:19-22).

This means that every member of the Church, whether Jew or Gentile, can read 1 - 2 Kings as part of *our* story. In particular, it's the bit of our story where we learn about the importance of king and temple.

A brief history of the king

Winston Churchill famously quipped that 'democracy is the worst form of Government except for all those other forms that have been tried from time to time',[7] which is a very clever way of saying that democracy is best.

But could monarchy be better?

Instinctively, many are wary of monarchy, particularly if the monarch isn't just a figurehead but wields real power. Our culture is suspicious of authority in general, and to locate it in just one individual seems intuitively foolish.

On the other hand, maybe monarchy is the one hope for unity. In the UK we've had two recent referenda that have split the population in two. The slightly less than half of Scots who voted for independence are frustrated with the slightly more than half who kept them British. The 48% who wanted to remain in the European Union were bitterly disappointed by the 52% who chose Brexit. What if these decisions were instead in the hands of a king whom *everyone* trusted? What if this king gave himself sacrificially for the good of his people? What if it were a lamb, not a wolf, on the throne?

We find in the pages of Scripture a very nuanced view of monarchy. It's neither rose-tinted nor entirely cynical.

Let's begin with the story of Saul, the first king of Israel (see 1 Samuel 8). The prophet Samuel had, in his old age, begun to delegate leadership responsibility to his sons, who didn't follow in his footsteps: they were absolute rotters. Bizarrely, the people then lobbied Samuel for a king, thereby seeking a form of government in which leadership automatically passes from father to son. Like players of the classic computer game, *Civilization*, they noticed that the surrounding countries had upgraded from 'Despotism' to 'Monarchy' and they didn't want to be left behind: 'Appoint for us a king to judge us like all the nations,' they said. The LORD took a dim view of their request, telling Samuel that 'they have rejected me from being king over them' (verse 7). They got what they deserved. King Saul was a disaster.

It's actually not the first time that a demand for a king had

---

[7] Elizabeth M. Knowles (ed.), *The Oxford Dictionary of Quotations* (Oxford: Oxford University Press, 1999), p. 216.

Introduction

terrible consequences. Impressed by Gideon's victory over the Midianites (which was really God's victory – all Gideon had to do was smash a jar and blow a trumpet) and wowed by his zero-tolerance approach to dissent, the people asked him to rule over them, followed by his son and his grandson; in other words, they too wanted to establish a monarchy (Judges 8:22). Gideon rightly dismissed the suggestion: 'I will not rule over you, and my son will not rule over you; the LORD will rule over you.' Nonetheless, the idea went to his head, and he soon demanded huge amounts of gold as tribute (which he melted down to make fancy underwear) and called his son Abimelech, which translated from Hebrew means 'my daddy is the king'.

'And if daddy is the king, then I want to be king next,' thought Abimelech, who was seventy-first in line to the throne – and so he murdered seventy of his brothers. The people of Shechem were mesmerised by his machismo and backed him. But one of his brothers survived the massacre to deliver a chilling message to his supporters:

> Listen to me, you leaders of Shechem, that God may listen to you. The trees once went out to anoint a king over them, and they said to the olive tree, 'Reign over us.' But the olive tree said to them, 'Shall I leave my abundance, by which gods and men are honoured, and go to hold sway over the trees?' And the trees said to the fig tree, 'You come and reign over us.' But the fig tree said to them, 'Shall I leave my sweetness and my good fruit and go to hold sway over the trees?' And the trees said to the vine, 'You come and reign over us.' But the vine said to them, 'Shall I leave my wine that cheers God and men and go to hold sway over the trees?' Then all the trees said to the bramble, 'You come and reign over us.' And the bramble said to the trees, 'If in good faith you are anointing me king over you, then come and take refuge in my shade, but if not, let fire come out of the bramble and devour the cedars of Lebanon.'
> (Judges 9:7–15)

The point of Jotham's fable is clear: a king can be a blessing, but only if chosen with pure motives. This is a critique that touches not only monarchy but also democracy, for the Shechemite electorate bore responsibility for the leader they elected.

Later in Judges comes a repeated refrain: 'In those days there was no king in Israel. Everyone did what was right in his own eyes' (17:6; 21:25; see also 18:1; 19:1).

It's often taken to mean that Israel would be better off with a king. But surely not if they get a king like Gideon or Abimelech, nor if they choose one 'in bad faith', nor as a tacit rejection of God as king over them. What would a *good* king look like?

After Genesis 14:18–20, where Abraham encountered the Christlike King of Salem (see Hebrews 7 and Psalm 110), and Genesis 17:6, where God promised to Abraham (and later to Isaac, 35:11) that 'kings shall come from you', and Genesis 49:10, where Jacob identified Judah (from whom Jesus traces his family tree) as the tribe from which 'the sceptre shall not depart', the most important reference to kingship comes in Deuteronomy. The first five books of the Bible (known as the 'Torah,' or Law) lay the foundation for all that follows, and the author of 1 - 2 Kings will expect us to know this paragraph inside out:

> When you come to the land that the LORD your God is giving you, and you possess it and dwell in it and then say, 'I will set a king over me, like all the nations that are around me,' you may indeed set a king over you whom the LORD your God will choose. One from among your brothers you shall set as king over you. You may not put a foreigner over you, who is not your brother. Only he must not acquire many horses for himself or cause the people to return to Egypt in order to acquire many horses, since the LORD has said to you, 'You shall never return that way again.' And he shall not acquire many wives for himself, lest his heart turn away, nor shall he acquire for himself excessive silver and gold.
>
> And when he sits on the throne of his kingdom, he shall write for himself in a book a copy of this law, approved by the

Levitical priests. And it shall be with him, and he shall read in it all the days of his life, that he may learn to fear the LORD his God by keeping all the words of this law and these statutes, and doing them, that his heart may not be lifted up above his brothers, and that he may not turn aside from the commandment, either to the right hand or to the left, so that he may continue long in his kingdom, he and his children, in Israel. (Deuteronomy 17:14–20)

Kingship was God's idea before it was a human idea. Long before the people entered the land and asked for a king, God anticipated the request and gave guidelines on how they should do kingship properly. The emphases on keeping God's law and not turning aside from his commandments are another way of saying that the king must recognise that God's authority comes above his own. God must be the king's king! And so the king mediates the rule of God, setting an example and directing the people to obey what God says (see Figure 3).

Figure 3 **Good king; bad king**

Introduction

Looking carefully at the list of dos and don'ts, we realised that asking for a king 'like all the nations' was not itself forbidden. Certainly, he mustn't have too much gold; he needs to limit the size of his stables; an excessive number of wives is not a good idea. But just because the country down the road has a king doesn't make it wrong for you to want one too … which means that we had misunderstood 1 Samuel 8 for years. We'd always assumed that the people's error was wanting to be like everyone else, but we needed to look again.

One problem is that they asked for a king to 'fight our battles' (1 Samuel 8:20). Later, Samuel reflects that it was 'when you saw that Nahash the king of the Ammonites came against you, you said to me, "No, but a king shall reign over us," *when the Lord your God was your king*' (1 Samuel 12:12, emphasis added). When the Creator of the universe is the head of your army, it's really not necessary to give a crown to a bloke with a sword. To distrust the God who has saved you so many times is to insult him.

However, a closer look at the structure of 1 Samuel 8 brought another issue to the fore. Samuel had issued an extended warning about the king they have chosen: he will 'take … take … take … take' (verses 10–18). But the people refused to 'obey the voice' of the prophet, and God handed them over to the consequences, telling the prophet to 'obey [the] voice' of the people (verses 19–22).[8] As we shall see often in 1 - 2 Kings, the way people respond to what God *says* is the ultimate indicator of their spiritual condition. When human voices prevail over the word of the Lord, adversity awaits.

After the disaster that was King Saul came the blessing that was King David. Although the Bible has already described some godly leaders (such as Abraham, Moses, Joshua, Samuel), David is the first godly *king* of Israel. And he is the one who receives the promise of an eternal kingdom.

This is supposed be a *Dig Deeper* book, and we realise to our horror that we've not yet used any of the tools. Time for you to

---

[8] Political historians will now discern an irony in the phrase *Vox populi, vox Dei*.

make a cup of tea, sit down at your workbench and get down to business.

> **Dig deeper exercise**
> Read 2 Samuel 7 a couple of times.
> Use the VOCABULARY TOOL, remembering its motto, 'Bible words have Bible meanings' (i.e., the words might have a technical sense that's not quite the same as how we use them in everyday life). Take the word 'house' for example. Can you see how it is being used *here*?

Alasdair took his wallet, went down to the bank and threw it in – splosh!

That sentence probably wrong-footed you, because of our mischievous play on the two meanings of 'bank' – a place to invest money or the side of a river. There's a similar word play in 2 Samuel 7 on the word 'house'. On the one hand, it refers to the temple that David longs to build for God (though he is told that his son will do so instead). On the other hand, it refers to a dynasty, a chain of royal succession that God will build for David (in the same way that students of British history refer to the House of Windsor or the House of Tudor).

Having unearthed something using the toolkit, we always need to consider the author's purpose in writing in this way: not just *what* but also *why*. Here the wordplay highlights that grace only flows in one direction.[9] At the very moment David tries to take the initiative to bless God, he is reminded that God is the one who blesses him (if you want further evidence, use the REPETITION TOOL to find out who does what in verses 8–14).

This promise is 'for ever' (verse 13, verse 16 twice). Even though Solomon fits the description of David's 'son' exactly – he comes from David's own body, he builds the Temple, he is disciplined but not stripped of his kingdom – people sometimes argue that it

---

9 John Piper makes this point emphatically in his book *Future Grace: The purifying power of the promises of God* (Colorado Springs, CO: Multnomah, 2012).

can't refer to him because he did not live for ever. Thus, they say, it must be about Jesus. While getting to Jesus is the right instinct, we need a bit more patience to travel *via* Solomon, rather than trying to bypass him. Let's read more carefully. The text doesn't say that any particular *king* will live forever. Rather, it is the 'throne' and 'house' and 'kingdom' that will be eternal. This promise is fulfilled by an unbroken succession of rulers who sit on the throne, beginning with Solomon. But this is a royal line that eventually reaches 'Eliud the father of Eleazar, and Eleazar the father of Matthan, and Matthan the father of Jacob, and Jacob the father of Joseph the husband of Mary, of whom Jesus was born, who is called Christ' (Matthew 1:15–16). It matters that Jesus comes in this family and comes to inherit these promises. And in *his* case, there will be no successor, for not only is he (like David and Solomon) king of an eternal kingdom, but (unlike them) he is an eternal king.[10]

David was a great king, the benchmark against whom later monarchs are assessed (e.g., 1 Kings 11:4; 15:3, 11). Like Moses before him, he worked in his youth as a shepherd, and the tending of sheep becomes a metaphor for the gentle care of people that God requires of a leader (e.g., Psalm 78:70–72). David mostly did the job well, probably because he acknowledged that 'the Lord is *my* shepherd' (Psalm 23:1, emphasis added). To repeat our slogan, God was the king's king.

Later kings failed terribly. Speaking through Ezekiel, and continuing with the shepherd metaphor, God expressed his anger at their negligence:

> The weak you have not strengthened, the sick you have not healed, the injured you have not bound up, the strayed you have not brought back, the lost you have not sought, and with force and harshness you have ruled them.
> (Ezekiel 34:4)

---

[10] The New Testament authors consistently refer to Jesus as 'Son of David', conscious that he is the heir of the 2 Samuel 7 promise of an eternal kingdom. But, significantly, they don't use that passage to argue that he is the eternal king. For that they cite Psalm 110.

Introduction

God then made an amazing promise: 'I myself will be the shepherd of the sheep ... I will seek the lost, and I will bring back the strayed, and I will bind up the injured, and I will strengthen the weak' (Ezekiel 34:15–16).

Confusingly, a few verses later, God says, 'I will set up over them one shepherd, my servant David, and he shall feed them: he shall feed them and be their shepherd' (Ezekiel 34:23).

So who is the promised shepherd? Is it God himself, or his messiah (David)? The passage's answer to this either-or question seems to be 'yes'! Could this be a glimpse of the Trinity at work? God does it, and his king does it, and yet somehow those amount to the same thing.

Hundreds of years later, Jesus of Nazareth announced the fulfilment of these prophecies when he said, 'I am the good shepherd. The good shepherd lays down his life for the sheep' (John 10:11).

Confusingly, a few verses later, Jesus also says that his Father holds the sheep in his hand (verse 29). So who is the promised shepherd? Is it God the Father, or his Son? It is exactly as Jesus revisits this Ezekiel paradox that he confirms our Trinitarian hunch: 'I and the Father are one' (John 10:30).

In summary, kingship was God's idea. Israel implemented it with bad motives and it was burdensome. God intervened with the 'house' promise and made it beautiful. Then what was beautiful became corrupted, but what was corrupted was redeemed through Jesus Christ. Now we pray in his name, 'Yours is the kingdom and the power and the glory, for ever and ever. Amen.'

> Rejoice, the Lord is King:
> Your Lord and King adore!
> Rejoice, give thanks and sing,
> And triumph evermore.
> Lift up your heart,
> Lift up your voice!
> Rejoice, again I say, rejoice![11]

---

11 From the hymn 'Rejoice, the Lord Is King', by Charles Wesley (1744, public domain).

A brief history of the temple

Let's turn now, more briefly, to trace the story of the temple. We begin in the garden of Eden, where God was present with his people, walking with them in the garden in the cool of the day (Genesis 3:8). This paradise was lost, and Adam and Eve were banished. But God acted with saving grace, and his people found themselves building a tabernacle in the wilderness by which God would again dwell with them (Exodus 25:8). This tent was glorious, not only in materials and craftsmanship, but in certain respects it was also deliberately Eden-like (something we explored in *Dig Deeper into Exodus*[12]). Later, after they had come to their permanent home in the land of sticky toffee pudding, the LORD made the 'house' promise, and told David that Solomon would 'build a house for my name' (2 Samuel 7:13).

Solomon's Temple, which we might call Tabernacle 2.0, would surely have been one of the seven wonders of the ancient world, had it not been destroyed before the list was compiled. It was breathtaking in artistry and scale and the sheer quantity of gold it contained, and it became the one place on earth of which God said, 'my name [will be] there' (1 Kings 9:3). But a few generations later, the southern tribes of Judah were carried off into exile by the Babylonians and the Temple was ransacked and burned. If you think of the combined humanitarian and archaeological devastation wrought by Islamic State, then you have something close, but in 2 Kings there was an added theological dimension: they were under the judgement of God.

Just as the prophets spoke of a better king, so they pointed forward to purified worship (e.g., Malachi 3:1-4) in a greater temple (e.g., Ezekiel 40–48). When Jesus of Nazareth came to the Temple, he purified it of false worship, and made an amazing promise: '"Destroy this temple, and in three days I will raise it up" … But he was speaking about the temple of his body' (John 2:19, 21).

---

12 Formerly published as Sach and Alldritt, *Dig Even Deeper*.

Introduction

King and Temple are important in 1 – 2 Kings, but they are also critical to understand where the universe is headed. In the final chapters of the Bible we read of a beautiful city paved with gold, with a throne at its centre. There isn't a temple, but only because 'its temple is the Lord God the Almighty and the Lamb' (Revelation 21:22). Reading 1 – 2 Kings, then, will help us to understand both the paradise that was lost and the greater paradise that we await in glorious hope. Let's add King and Temple to our diagram (see Figure 4).

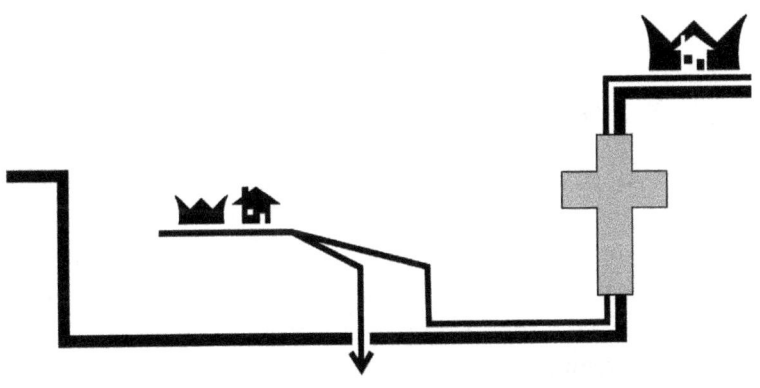

Figure 4 **King and Temple**

The prophetic word

A third key theme in 1 – 2 Kings is the fulfilment of God's word. Again and again God speaks through a prophet to announce what will later come to pass. It always comes to pass. Even when there is a delay, sometimes of more than a generation. Even when powerful men or women do their best to thwart it.

The prophets themselves are key characters in the narrative. Some are unnamed (simply 'a man of God'), some enjoy the limelight for a scene or two (such as Micaiah, Jonah, Isaiah), and two would have their faces on the poster and their names first in the opening credits: Elijah and Elisha dominate the central section of Kings, and in various ways they anticipate the ministries of John the Baptist and the Lord Jesus.

Introduction

Often, Christians teach doctrine from the New Testament letters. We might expect a seminar on the doctrine of Scripture to focus on passages like 2 Timothy 3:14–17 or 2 Peter 1:16–21, and a church weekend away on God's sovereignty to expound Ephesians 1 and Romans 9. That's well and good. But God reveals himself in Old Testament narrative too, and arguably there is no more compelling or comforting testimony to the infallibility of God's word and completeness of his control than watching history unfold exactly as he said it would.

Applying the Old Testament

In the last couple of years, both of our churches have done a Bible Overview in small groups. To help people navigate between the world of the Old Testament and our own, we gave each group three special props.

The *Ace of Immutability* (a playing card on which someone had written Malachi 3:6, 'I the LORD do not change', and Hebrews 13:8, 'Jesus Christ is the same yesterday and today and forever'). This was intended to remind us that anything we learn about God in the Old Testament is still true about God today. Jim Packer puts the point brilliantly:

> Our Bible reading takes us into what, for us, is quite a new world – namely, the Near Eastern world as it was thousands of years ago, primitive and barbaric, agricultural and unmechanised ... It is all intensely interesting, but it all seems very far away. It all belongs to *that* world, not to *this* world ... We cannot see how the two worlds link up, and hence again and again we find ourselves feeling that the things we read about in the Bible can have no application to us ... The link is God himself. For the God with whom they had to do is the same God with whom we have to do. We could sharpen the point by saying, *exactly* the same God; for God does not change in the least particular. Thus it appears that the truth on which we must dwell in order to dispel this feeling that there is an

Introduction

unbridgeable gulf between the position of men and women in Bible times and our own, is the truth of God's *immutability*.[13]

The *Scroll of Time* (a roll of paper tied up with a ribbon on which people would sketch an outline of each week's Bible passage, so that eventually it became a very long comic strip or movie storyboard). This was intended to remind us that the whole Bible is a single narrative that only makes sense if read in order. The point of giving you a *brief history of king and temple*, above, was to sketch out part of this scroll so you know where to place the events of 1 – 2 Kings. To apply them correctly to ourselves, we need to take account of the fact that we join the story *later*, after some very significant plot developments.

The *Envelope of Fulfilment* (an envelope into which the leader had slipped one or two New Testament verses that allude directly to the Old Testament passage we were studying that week). This was intended to remind us that God has arranged history such that things, people and events that come later are often foreshadowed by those that come before. The technical word for it is typology. For example, when a Christian reads of the blood of the Passover lamb splattered on the door (Exodus 12), they can't help but think of the blood of the Lamb with a capital L. When a Christian reads that the remedy for being bitten by venomous snakes is to look at a bronze snake lifted up on a pole (Numbers 21:4–9), Jesus tells us to draw the parallel with his own lifting up to save us from perishing (John 3:14–16). When a Christian reads that King David is betrayed by one close to him, immediately after a kiss (2 Samuel 14:33 – 15:14), their thoughts will inevitably turn to Judas Iscariot (Luke 22:47–8). If the *Scroll of Time* reminds us that texts should ordinarily be read in chronological order, then typology is the 'hyperlink' – if you remember those from the early days of the internet – inviting us occasionally to jump ahead in the story. In careless hands, the typological becomes the whatever-you-want-ological, of which we shall share a couple of eyebrow-raising examples. But if we let the biblical authors guide us, then the *Envelope of Fulfilment* will

---

13 J. I. Packer, *Knowing God* (London: Hodder and Stoughton, 1993), pp. 83–4.

Introduction

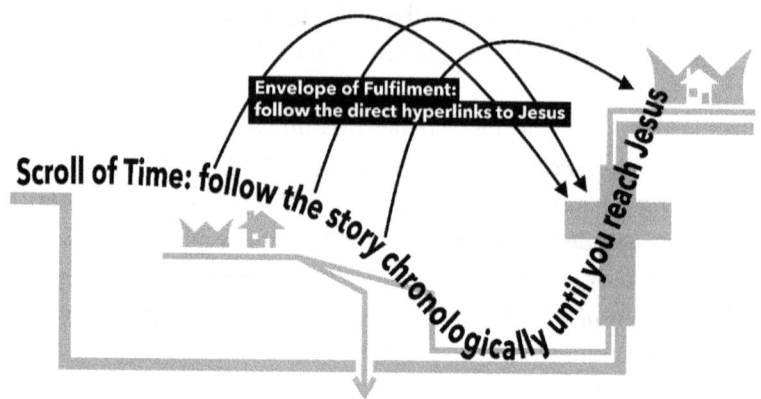

Figure 5 **Two 'routes' from then to us**

provide us with plenty of opportunities to see Jesus in 1 – 2 Kings (see Figure 5).

You might think our threefold approach was quite a complicated way of doing a Bible Overview. Some of our friends eschew the hyperlinks and insist on reading strictly in chronological order, never skipping ahead. But that can make for quite a pessimistic reading of the Old Testament:

> Jesus isn't here yet. We are still waiting for Jesus. They're in a mess because they need Jesus. This temporary solution won't really fix things because it's not Jesus. Still no Jesus. FINALLY, JESUS!

Whereas the typological strands help us to be a bit more glass half full:

> Here is something a bit like Jesus. And we can see Jesus prefigured here too. Sure, this bit of the story is a mess but with just a hint of Jesus. And this temporary solution is very Jesus-like. And he's here too.

To be fair to our pessimistic friends, we have to admit that the overall shape of 1 – 2 Kings *is* gloomy. It begins with the glory of

Solomon's Temple and ends with exile and a lot of death. But there are wonderful glimpses of Christ throughout. It's a dark downward spiral studded with bright diamonds of grace.

Who were the first readers and does it matter?

On the Cornhill Training Course, where I (Andrew) was formerly a student and am now a tutor, we teach the importance of 'going back to Corinth'. To understand 1 Corinthians properly, we must hear it as it would have been heard by first-century Corinthian ears. Only then can we use the AUTHOR'S PURPOSE TOOL and understand why Paul wrote what he wrote. For example, the Corinthians were easily impressed with rhetoric and cleverness. That led to rivalry as each faction in the church had a different favourite preacher. And so Paul countered it by teaching that at the cross God deliberately 'made foolish the wisdom of the world' (1:20). Or again, they had bought into the philosophy of Plato that souls were immortal but bodies disposable. That led to sexual immorality, as people thought that what you did with your body didn't matter. And so Paul countered it by explaining how the bodily resurrection of Jesus guarantees the resurrection of our bodies.

To understand 1 Corinthians, we go back to Corinth. To understand Ephesians, we go back to Ephesus. So how does this apply to reading 1 – 2 Kings? The first answer is that we must go back to *Babylon*. That's not where most of the action is set – the events of 1 – 2 Kings take place mainly within Israel, with a couple of forays across the border to places like Sidon and Syria – but it's where the book *ends*, and therefore where it would have been published and first read. Granted, the author of the completed volume had earlier sources to draw on,[14] but he was writing for his contemporaries in captivity in a foreign land.

---

14 There are thirty-six references in 1 – 2 Kings to the 'Book of the Chronicles of the Kings of Israel' or the 'Book of the Chronicles of the Kings of Judah' (e.g., 1 Kings 14:19, 29). These earlier sources are not to be confused with the biblical book of Chronicles, which was written later, in the days of Ezra, when the Israelites returned from exile.

Introduction

So imagine yourself sitting down with Ezekiel 'among the exiles by the Chebar canal' (Ezekiel 1:1), listening to the *original* of Psalm 137 (Boney M's cover version, one of the top-selling UK singles of all time, wouldn't be recorded for another 2,570 years). Hot off the press – though they didn't have printing presses yet, so hot from the prophet's pen – comes the book of 1 – 2 Kings. You read of a glorious Temple, now in ruins. You read of the majesty of Israel's royal family, now in prison. These chapters don't tell you how things *are* but how they *were*. Your reading is full of wistfulness and regret: 'How did we throw all of this away?'

Yet you are kept from despair by the hyperlinks of hope. These are often clearer with the benefit of hindsight, and undoubtedly a New Testament reader with an *Envelope of Fulfilment* sees more than Old Testament saints would have done. But it's important to realise that 1 – 2 Kings is itself prophetic, forward-looking. The apostles didn't read into it something extra that wasn't there in the Jewish Scriptures, but shone a brighter light on what had been before everyone's noses all along (see Acts 2:30–31; Romans 16:25–6; 1 Peter 1:9–10; 2 Peter 1:19). The first readers had known ever since Moses' day that they would be exiled but that God would ultimately have mercy on them and gather them to himself (Deuteronomy 30:1–14; compare 1 Kings 8:46–53). When they discovered that God's prophets had raised the dead, they presumably wondered if they would do so again (1 Kings 17:17–24; 2 Kings 4:18–37; 8:5; 13:21).

There is another perspective, though. Rather than simply reading the story retrospectively, as if in Babylon looking back, we can also experience the events *as they unfold*, as if viewing the action from a GoPro strapped to the forehead of one of the characters. Sam Mendes won the Oscar for best cinematography for doing something similar in *1917* (with the added flair of filming the entire movie as if it were a single continuous shot). Or consider another Academy Award winner, James Cameron's *Titanic*.[15] You'd think that knowing in advance how the story ends would ruin the

---

15 *1917*, directed by Sam Mendes (2019); *Titanic*, directed by James Cameron (1997).

Introduction

suspense (spoiler alert: the ship sinks!), yet somehow we are still carried on an emotional roller coaster. We still enjoy the glamour of the ballroom. We still feel the romantic tension – will they? won't they? – between Leonardo DiCaprio and Kate Winslet. We still feel indignant at Cal's arrogance. And *then* we hit the iceberg, and there is panic, and our hero drowns and we mourn him.

A few subtle features of 1 – 2 Kings made us realise we *must* read it in this kind of way. For example, in describing the Temple, 1 Kings 8:8 tells us that the poles on the ark of the covenant were so long they could be seen from the Holy Place *'to this day'*, even though the Temple was destroyed at the end of 2 Kings and so the poles cannot have been there on the day of publication. Similarly, 1 Kings 12:19 informs the reader after the split of the kingdom that *'Israel has been in rebellion against the house of David to this day'*, despite the fact that the ten northern tribes had been scattered into exile and lost.

Thus, even if we know the final outcome of the plot, we ought not to jump ahead. Let's follow the story as the author tells it.

Are you ready?

If you've read the previous *Dig Deeper* books, you'll know this is the point where we ask you to do something that authors don't normally do: put this book down and ignore it until you've finished reading another much better book. We mean you should read 1 – 2 Kings itself. Look out for big themes; try to sketch out a rough structure; play the *Ace of Immutability*, write out a timeline on a scroll and hide some New Testament verses in an envelope. Only then will you be ready to turn the page and begin the adventure with us ...

Contents page (with a difference)

This isn't so much a contents page as a contents chapter. We are going to explain why we split up 1 – 2 Kings the way that we have.

You might think that the obvious break is between 1 Kings and 2 Kings, but this isn't very helpful at all. In the original Hebrew, 1 – 2 Kings comprise a single volume, and 1 Kings ends (just because they didn't make scrolls long enough?) mid-way through the story of Ahaziah. We are expected to read on without a break.

The easiest structural markers to spot are the coronations and obituaries. At the beginning of a king's reign we are often told:[1]

- How to keep in sync with the chronology across the border ('In the twenty-seventh year of Jeroboam, king of Israel …')
- His name and his father's name ('… Azariah the son of Amaziah, king of Judah, began to reign.')
- How long he reigned ('And he reigned for fifty-two years in Jerusalem.')
- His mother's name ('His mother's name was Jecoliah of Jerusalem.')
- Whether he was a goodie or a baddie ('And he did what was right in the eyes of the LORD.')

And at the end of his reign we are told:

- How long he reigned, and whether he was a goodie or a baddie, if we weren't told earlier
- Where to find out more ('Now the rest of the acts of Azariah …

---

[1] This example is from 2 Kings 15:1–7.

Contents page (with a difference)

are they not written in the Book of the Chronicles of the Kings of Judah?')
- Where he is buried ('And Azariah slept with his fathers, and they buried him with his fathers in the city of David.')
- Who succeeded him ('Jotham his son reigned in his place.')

So it's a piece of cake to separate the sovereigns. But it's not going to make sense to go for one section per king, because the author covers them at such different speeds. Some get multiple chapters to themselves, the camera moving slowly enough to take in many details, even facial expressions (e.g., 1 Kings 20:43). At other times the author steps on the gas and we whizz past several reigns in a single chapter, a bit like a montage in a film.

From Rehoboam onwards, the kingdom splits in two, Israel to the north and Judah to the south. You might think we should deal with one province and then the other, but the author doesn't quite do that. It will be significant to notice how he tells the two stories in parallel, and sometimes juxtaposes them (such as when Jehoshaphat, king of Judah, features in a section about Ahab, king of Israel, in 1 Kings 22 and again in 2 Kings 3).

Finally, the prophets Elijah and Elisha are more important than the kings they serve under, and so they get a section each to themselves.

As we begin to look at the text in detail we'll discover further relationships between sections, sandwiches, palistrophes, etc. But that can wait for now. Here's the contents page:

The Bible toolkit	1
Introduction	3
Contents page (with a difference) (you are here!)	26

SOLOMON

Long live King Solomon (1 Kings 1 – 2)	33
The wisdom of Solomon (1 Kings 3 – 4)	39

Contents page (with a difference)

The gold telephone (1 Kings 5 – 8)	47
It took her breath away (1 Kings 9 – 10)	58
Trouble and strife x700 (1 Kings 11:1–25)	64

THE DIVIDED KINGDOM

1 Kings 11:26 – 12:24 (1 Kings 11:26 – 12:24)	73
The lion, the altar and the failed disguise (1 Kings 12:25 – 14:20)	79
Good king, bad king (1 Kings 14:21 – 16:28)	86

ELIJAH

Yahweh vs Baal: round 1 (1 Kings 16:29 – 17:24)	93
Yahweh vs Baal: round 2 (1 Kings 18)	99
The still, small voice (1 Kings 19)	105
The owardice of King Ahab (1 Kings 20 – 21)	112
The prophet who refused to scratch where they itched (1 Kings 22:1–50)	118
Up and down and down and up (1 Kings 22:51 – 2 Kings 1:18)	124

ELISHA

Swing low, sweet chariot (2 Kings 2)	131
A nation saved (2 Kings 3)	136
A remnant saved (2 Kings 4)	142
A Gentile saved (2 Kings 5)	148
Blindness and sight (2 Kings 6:1 – 8:6)	156
God's assassins (2 Kings 8:7 – 10:31)	160

THE DOWNWARD SPIRAL

The house in the house (2 Kings 11 – 12)	169
The beginning of the end (2 Kings 13:1 – 17:5)	176
The fall of Israel (2 Kings 17:6–41)	184

Contents page (with a difference)

The king who trusted God (2 Kings 18 – 19)	189
Turning back the sundial (2 Kings 20)	196
The beginning of the end (Part 2): too little, too late (2 Kings 21:1 – 23:30)	202
The fall of Judah (2 Kings 23:31 – 25:26)	210
Coda (2 Kings 25:27–30)	213
Scripture and other copyright acknowledgements	216

SOLOMON

Long live King Solomon

1 Kings 1 – 2

Now would be a good time to pray for God's help as you listen to his word, and then to read 1 Kings 1 – 2.

Whose throne is it anyway? (1 Kings 1)

I (Andrew) got an A grade in my GSCE biology exam. This is partly, I admit, owing to the unusually effective teaching methods of Mrs … (actually it may be best to preserve her anonymity!). One day, just before a practical exam in which we were instructed to soak strips of beetroot in different saline solutions and observe them bend due to osmosis, she announced that for the first 'completely unrelated' five minutes of the lesson, we would spend time revising … osmosis. Unsurprisingly, we all did rather well.

Like the osmosis exam, 1 Kings chapter 1 contains some ideas that might catch us out if we haven't recently studied the life of King David. Following the example of Mrs X, we thought we would extend to you the benefits of what we might call 'highly targeted revision'.

You might find it useful to know that:

- King David's accession to the throne was contested by a fierce rival (called Ish-bosheth).
- His most important courtiers were Zadok the priest, Nathan the prophet, Benaiah and the mighty men.
- In later life he faced another rival, his own son Absalom, who was famed for his dashing good looks.

Now we're ready to begin!

Solomon

King David is an old man. It's time to find a successor (REPETITION TOOL: the phrase 'sit on the throne' is repeated some nine times, and the question of who will do so is the dominant idea of the chapter). Adonijah, the eldest son, naturally steps forward. But several alarm bells sound for the well-informed reader.

> **Dig deeper exercise**
> Read verses 5–10 again.
> Given our use of the CONTEXT TOOL above, what now troubles you about Adonijah?
> - Consider his appearance (verse 6).
> - Consider his guest list (verses 8, 10; compare with verse 26).

In 1:11–27, the illegitimacy of Adonijah's claim becomes more explicit: David had promised that Solomon would succeed him (verses 13, 17, 27). Some commentaries speculate that, because we haven't read of this promise previously in the biblical narrative, it was invented out of thin air by a scheming Nathan; he and his accomplice Bathsheba (Solomon's ambitious tiger mum) then repeated it to a senile old David in the hope he would remember it as his own. There are no hints of this in the text. If anyone has invented anything out of thin air, it's these commentators!

Let's try to stick closer to what the chapter actually says. We are given no reason to doubt the integrity of the LORD's prophet, but we *are* told at length how he and Bathsheba had to prod David into action. Then there is the curious detail that despite being given a 'very beautiful' woman as a hot-water bottle, David didn't get up to anything sexual with her (verse 4). Why are we told this? To emphasise his moral purity? Maybe, but why say that *here*? Or to underline his lack of libido? That makes more sense because it all builds into a consistent picture: David is old and cold; his libido is dead; his memory is fuzzy; he's in no fit state to govern the country and the rightful succession looks very precarious. No wonder Adonijah takes a punt. Will the LORD intervene?

Suddenly within a few quick paragraphs, everything is resolved. David has at last announced Solomon as his successor. Solomon has been anointed with much celebration. Adonijah has heard the news, relinquished his claim to the throne and paid homage to the new king.

It's significant that, where Adonijah had grasped at power, exalting himself, Solomon was passive. He didn't work to overthrow his rival or promote his own candidacy. He received the kingdom by grace. In this respect, his succession to the throne is remarkably similar to his father's. David had done little to defeat his rival Ish-bosheth, yet emerged as the uncontested king of a united Israel. The connection is strengthened when we discover that the oath David swore over Solomon in 1:29 – 'As the LORD lives, who has redeemed my soul out of every adversity' – is identical to one he swore just before the start of his own reign in 2 Samuel 4:9.

In these various ways, we are shown that the passing of the kingdom from David to Solomon is ultimately God's doing. As David himself put it, 'Blessed be the LORD, the God of Israel, who has granted someone to sit on my throne this day' (verse 48).

Passing on the ~~baton~~ sceptre (1 Kings 2:1–12)

Given the ups and downs of David's own kingship, he's understandably keen that his son doesn't make the same mistakes. So he gives Solomon a pep talk, telling him to be a good boy in order 'that the LORD may establish his word that he spoke concerning me, saying …'

How do you expect him to complete the sentence? It sounds like he's about to quote the famous kingdom promise from 2 Samuel 7. And he does quote it – kind of. But because we are careful users of the QUOTATION/ALLUSION TOOL, we checked the original and noticed that David has put a different gloss on it (see Table 2).

This sets up an important tension that will run throughout 1 – 2 Kings. How will God's promises fare if the king goes off the rails? Is

Original version (2 Samuel 7:12–18)	David's version (1 Kings 2:4)
'When your days are fulfilled and you lie down with your fathers, I will raise up your offspring after you, who shall come from your body . . . When he commits iniquity, I will discipline him with the rod of men, with the stripes of the sons of men, but my steadfast love will not depart from him . . . And your house and your kingdom shall be made sure for ever before me.'	'If your sons pay close attention to their way, to walk before me in faithfulness with all their heart and with all their soul, you shall not lack a man on the throne of Israel.'
The continuation of the kingdom seems guaranteed even if there is disobedience.	The continuation of the kingdom seems conditional on obedience.
For this note of unconditionality, see also 1 Kings 11:36; 15:4; 2 Kings 8:19.	For this note of conditionality, see also 1 Kings 3:6; 6:12–13; 8:25; 9:4, 6-7.

Table 2 **Conditional or unconditional?**

the 'for ever' nature of the promise secure, or do disobedient rulers jeopardise everything?

Next, we get a paragraph detailing the judgement that Solomon must mete out on various characters (2:5-9), a theme that spills over into the next section.

Then the author brings the section to a close with a summary in 2:10–12. As we read through the book we will become very familiar with this kind of epitaph: 'King such and such slept with his fathers; he reigned for x years; so and so reigned in his place.' This one is slightly different from the others, as we are told that Solomon 'sat on the throne' of David (one last repetition of that key phrase) and that 'his kingdom was firmly established'.

Solomon executes judgement (1 Kings 2:13–46)

Maybe you've come across Bible Project – a collection of helpful YouTube videos with amazingly high production values. They reckon that Solomon's reign is 'not off to a good start' because of

1 Kings 1 – 2

what they describe as 'a whole series of *political* assassinations'.[1] Certainly he does bump quite a few people off, but we're not sure they are right to dismiss this as a godless Machiavellian move. Various clues in the text suggest that Solomon is in fact acting justly, in a way that fulfils prophecy and embodies godly wisdom.

First up is Adonijah (2:13–25). He was warned back in 1:52, 'If he will show himself a worthy man, not one of his hairs shall fall to the earth, but if wickedness is found in him, he shall die.' How foolish of him, then, to court Abishag, the woman who had been so intimate with King David (1:2–4). It looks like a power play, and it costs him his life.

Next, Abiathar the priest (2:26–7), who together with Joab 'helped' Adonijah in his earlier bid for power (see 1:7). He is banished, in fulfilment of a word God spoke back in 1 Samuel 2:27–36.

Next, Joab (2:28–35) who, although loyal to David during his lifetime, had been morally unscrupulous. In the end, it is Joab's part in supporting Adonijah that gives Solomon reason to sign his death warrant.

Finally, Shimei (2:36–46), a horrid character who, at David's lowest point, pursued him down a valley, cursing and hurling stones (2 Samuel 16:13). He is placed under house arrest (2:36), but after three years saddles his donkey and sets off on a journey. For breaking the terms of his containment, he is executed.

Using the CONTEXT TOOL, we observe that in executing Joab and Shimei, Solomon was following the advice of King David:

> Act therefore according to your wisdom, but do not let his grey head go down to Sheol in peace.
> (1 Kings 2:6)

> Do not hold him guiltless, for you are a wise man. You will know what you ought to do to him, and you shall bring his grey head down with blood to Sheol.
> (1 Kings 2:9).

---

[1] '1&2 Kings', Bible Project: bibleproject.com/explore/video/kings (accessed 26 July 2024).

Then with the other hand we pick up the REPETITION TOOL and spot that both of David's instructions call for Solomon's *wisdom*, which means acting rightly and justly in a given situation (more about this in the next chapter).

All of this suggests the author wants us to see the executions as a legitimate application of the rule of law rather than nefarious political manoeuvrings. Accordingly, his summary is entirely positive: 'So the kingdom was established in the hand of Solomon' (2:46).

The coronation of the King of kings

The ultimate 'Son of David' is not Solomon but the Lord Jesus, so as we read this succession narrative we think naturally of him. He is the one whose kingdom the LORD will ultimately establish, though he did not grasp at it (see Philippians 2:5–11). He is the one for whom the note of conditionality does not threaten the promise, for he perfectly obeyed God's law. He is the one who is supremely wise and whose opponents will not stand.

Let's close with a famous coronation hymn:

Now therefore, O kings, be wise;
    be warned, O rulers of the earth.
Serve the LORD with fear,
    and rejoice with trembling.
Kiss the Son,
    lest he be angry, and you perish in the way,
    for his wrath is quickly kindled.
Blessed are all who take refuge in him.
(Psalm 2:10–12)

The wisdom of Solomon
1 Kings 3 – 4

A quick reminder that now would be a good time to pray for God's help as you listen to his word, and then to read 1 Kings 3 – 4. We won't keep saying it, but please keep doing it!

Off to a bad start? (1 Kings 3:1–4)

Imagine arriving at your driving test only to realise that you are wearing the wrong glasses. In your nervousness you then turn on the windscreen wipers instead of the ignition and mistake the examiner's knee for the gearstick. It doesn't look promising. The same might be said for the first four verses of 1 Kings 3. Immediately after being told that 'the kingdom was established in the hand of Solomon' (2:46b), we are given a sketch of his reign that gives us misgivings. The REPETITION TOOL sniffs out the issue:

> 'The people were sacrificing at the high places.'

> 'Solomon … sacrificed and made offerings at the high places.'

> 'The king went to Gibeon to sacrifice there, for that was the great high place.'

Sacrificing at high places is forbidden in the law of Moses (see Deuteronomy 12:1–14). Some have argued that this prohibition didn't come into force until the Temple was built, or that Gibeon might be legit because the tabernacle was there (2 Chronicles 1:3). However, the author of 1 Kings signals his disapproval in verse 3, where he contrasts sacrifices at high places with the love for God that otherwise characterised Solomon.

Two other details in the opening paragraph spell trouble, but we perceive it only with the benefit of hindsight. First, Solomon takes an Egyptian wife; later, many foreign wives will be responsible for the further proliferation of high places and the turning of his heart away from the LORD (11:1–8). Second, he builds 'his own house and the house of the LORD'. Later, the author will reveal that the royal palace took twice as long as the Temple, perhaps indicating skewed priorities (6:38; 7:1).

But we mustn't get ahead of the author, who has chosen to delay these criticisms until much later in his account. As John Woodhouse comments, 'qualms about [the] foreign marriage are not shared … by our narrator *at this point*'.[1] For the most part Solomon is presented as a goodie, and the next scene makes that all the clearer.

Be careful what you wish for (1 Kings 3:5 – 4:34)

To cheer yourself up after your failed driving test, you decide to go for some retail therapy. Browsing in a charity shop, you happen upon an old brass lamp, which you think might polish up smartly. Giving it a little rub with your handkerchief, you are surprised to see a genie appear and promptly offer you three wishes.

That *really* would be surprising, because genies don't exist. But God does exist, and amazingly he appears to Solomon and gives him the opportunity to ask for whatever he wants. Pause for a moment and consider how astonishing this is. The Creator of the universe effectively offers a blank cheque to a mere man.

It's even more remarkable that, given the dodgy goings-on at Gibeon (3:4), this mind-blowing offer is made 'at Gibeon' (verse 5). God is kind when Solomon least deserves it. Such grace!

---

1 John Woodhouse, *1 Kings: Power, politics and the hope of the world* (Wheaton, IL: Crossway, 2018), p. 115. Italics original.

1 Kings 3 – 4

Put yourself in Solomon's shoes for a moment – what would you choose? A holiday in Barbados? A penthouse in Manhattan? A Ferrari (though that wouldn't be much use unless you pass your test)? Solomon asks for none of these, but rather for *wisdom*, and this becomes the central theme.

> ### Dig deeper exercise
> The VOCABULARY TOOL bears the inscription 'Bible words have Bible meanings', and so we need to stop and ask what 'wisdom' means. Is it just about being clever? Is Solomon simply better than anyone else at working out which arrangement of abstract shapes belongs next in the sequence in an IQ test? See if you can write a biblical definition based on how the word is used in these chapters.
> Wisdom / ˈwɪzdəm/ (noun): that quality in a person characterised by: _____ and _____ and _____ and _____ and _____ and _____ and _____.

How did you get on? Here is our attempt. Wisdom is that quality in a person characterised by:

- Humility. Unlike so many clever people in the world, Solomon doesn't think of himself as a self-made man. He recognises that all he is and all he has was *given* (verses 6–7a).[2] His autobiography refers to 'a little child' who doesn't 'know how to go out or come in' (verse 7b). The wise man (or woman) thinks little of himself.[3]
- Moral judgement. In a James Bond movie you can have an 'evil genius', but in the Bible's thinking that's a contradiction in terms. To be wise is to be moral, to be able to 'discern between

---

[2] Recognising grace is a wonderful antidote to pride. We recommend including in your biblical medicine cabinet the following anti-inflammatory. Dosage: one verse, to be taken whenever you are puffed up. Active ingredient: 1 Corinthians 4:7.

[3] We will speak mainly of the wise man because this is the usual phrase in the Bible, and because Solomon the archetype was male. But these qualities are also admirable in a woman.

good and evil' (verse 9), 'discern what is right' (verse 11), 'do justice' (verse 28). The wise man prizes what is good.
- Altruism. The businessman undertakes an MBA as part of his '*personal* career development' (we barely notice the selfishness inherent in the phrase). Conversely, Solomon seeks wisdom for the good of the 'great people' he must govern (verses 8–9). The wise man looks not only to his own interests but also to the interests of others.

Then we read that 'it pleased the Lord that Solomon had asked this' (verse 10). Asking for wisdom was the right call. You might even say it was wise to ask for wisdom! In particular, God was delighted that he asked for it *rather than* long life, riches and military success (verse 11), and in response it was given *together with* these things. Solomon later reflected on this:

> Blessed is the one who finds wisdom,
>   and the one who gets understanding,
> for the gain from her is better than gain from silver
>   and her profit better than gold.
> She is more precious than jewels,
>   and nothing you desire can compare with her.
> Long life is in her right hand;
>   in her left hand are riches and honour.
> (Proverbs 3:13–16)

As the lady in the charity shop clocks up 'one brass lamp' on the cash register, another woman bursts in and accuses her of stealing her baby. They appeal to you to adjudicate. It's obvious the situation may escalate and there's no time for DNA tests or an appearance on *The Jeremy Kyle Show*. Can you think of a quick and easy way to resolve the dispute using only the antique sword in the window?

Solomon's answer is deservedly famous. The showcase trial of the almost-halved baby proves that Solomon has received the gift he asked for. No one is in any doubt that 'the wisdom of God was in him to do justice' (verse 28).

1 Kings 3 – 4

We can now fill out our definition of 'wisdom' still further. It is:

- Practical. There is a certain esoteric pleasure in knowing that 1729 is 'the smallest number expressible as a sum of two cubes in two different ways'.[4] But Solomon's wisdom isn't about thinking in the abstract; he acts to resolve the problems of real life. The wise man affects other people's fortunes profoundly.
- Equitable. The insights of the life coach are available only to the deep-pocketed elite. But isn't it beautiful that the blessing of Solomon's wisdom extends even to a prostitute (verse 16)? The wise person cares for those in the gutter.

Time for the 'SO WHAT?!' TOOL. We have seen that true wisdom is characterised by humility, moral judgement and altruism. Furthermore, it is practical and equitable. So let's repent of smug cleverness and seek these qualities of godly wisdom. And when God appears to us in a dream, let's ask for wisdom above riches …

… knowing that he will make us rich as well? Oops. Hopefully you're smelling a rat. Indeed, not only a rat but that whole stinking sewer known as the Prosperity Gospel. Something has gone wrong, but we have to dig a bit deeper to figure out exactly what.

It's right that Christians should seek wisdom from God. In fact, the book of James says explicitly, 'If any of you lacks wisdom, let him ask God, who gives generously to all without reproach, and it will be given him' (James 1:5). He contrasts 'the wisdom from above [which] is first pure, then peaceable, gentle, open to reason, full of mercy and good fruits, impartial and sincere' with 'earthly wisdom' which springs from 'bitter jealousy and selfish ambition in your hearts' (James 3:14–17). We made a similar comparison above.

However, skilled toolkit users, armed with the AUTHOR'S PURPOSE TOOL, will ask whether James's purpose is the same as

---

4 As the mathematician Ramanujan famously remarked to his friend Hardy, who had caught cab number 1729 to visit him one day. See G. H. Hardy, *Ramanujan* (London: Cambridge University Press, 1940), p. 12.

the purpose of 1 – 2 Kings. James is telling us about the blessing of wisdom for the individual Christian; 1 Kings is telling us about the blessing of a wise *king*.

Next, we reach for the 'WHO AM I?' TOOL, which reminds us not to step automatically into Solomon's shoes. Did God appear to every Israelite in a dream, offering them a wish? Did he give all of them wisdom to govern the people? Did every one of them act as a judge of the two prostitutes? Did every one of them become enormously rich? No. Only Solomon. Who am I? I am not Solomon. I am not the king.

Chapter 4 shows that a wise and prosperous king is good news for every single one of his subjects, and that's where I fit in. I am a citizen of the kingdom of heaven, whose king God has chosen! But before we think about the implications for our own day, let's linger a little longer in the tenth century BC and allow the author to show us the glory of God's kingdom on earth.

He begins with a description of Solomon's Cabinet (verses 1–6) and local government officials (verses 7–19), and how they take turns to provide for his household. The author deliberately sidesteps the issue of the tax burden (compare 12:4) to emphasise the universal prosperity the people enjoyed: 'Judah and Israel were as many as the sand by the sea. They ate and drank and were happy' (verse 20).

Next we are told of Solomon's incredible prosperity and lavish dining habits. We are both partial to a ribeye steak or perhaps a rack of lamb as a special treat. Here we are talking thirty whole cows and a hundred sheep *per day* (verses 22–3)! What?! This makes the film *Supersize Me* look like a diet plan![5] How obese was this guy? But look at verse 27. The food was not for the king alone, but also for the many who shared his table. The king's blessings overflowed to those around him.

We close (verses 29–34) with a climactic celebration of Solomon's wisdom. This is a good place to use the TONE AND FEEL TOOL, since the aim is not necessarily to add theological data, but to seek to

---

5 *Supersize Me*, directed by Morgan Spurlock (2004).

appreciate the force and weight of what's already been said. We need to be attuned to the author's use of metaphor, allusion and so on, as he underlines just how wise Solomon was:

- He compares his breadth of mind with 'the sand on the seashore' (verse 29). The metaphor is effective at describing vast quantity, but surely it's also significant that it's a *reused* metaphor from earlier in the Bible story (QUOTATION/ALLUSION TOOL: Genesis 22:17; 32:12; compare 1 Kings 4:20), and brings with it overtones of God's covenant-faithfulness.
- He gives examples of well-known wise men of the day, and assures us that Solomon trumps them (verse 31): 'Ethan the Ezrahite? Mahol's sons? Yeah, they are fairly wise I suppose, but not a patch on Solomon.' A modern equivalent might be 'Gary Kasparov? Magnus Carlsen? Solomon would checkmate them in fewer than twenty moves.'
- He is specific about Solomon's literary output: three thousand proverbs and (lest you thought he was just picking a ballpark round number) one thousand *and five* songs (verse 32).
- He refers to Solomon's knowledge of the natural world (verse 33) in a way that reminds most people of David Attenborough, but should make us think of Adam, back in the garden of Eden, before it all went wrong. Earlier we are told that Solomon 'ruled' (verse 21) and 'had dominion' (verse 24), which is also evocative of Genesis 1 – 2.

Notice how far wisdom's reputation extends: 'people of all nations came to hear the wisdom of Solomon' (verse 34). This was the Golden Age of Israel, a time of great blessing not only for the Israelites themselves, but also for the whole world. Later generations would look back at this period with wistful nostalgia. When the prophet Micah later tells a disheartened people that 'it shall come to pass in the latter days that … they shall sit every man under his vine and under his fig tree' (Micah 4:1, 4; see also Zechariah 3:10), he is harking back to 1 Kings 4:25, when 'Judah and Israel lived in safety, from Dan even to Beersheba [the equivalent of 'from John

O'Groats to Land's End'], every man under his vine and under his fig tree, all the days of Solomon'.

From this we can add final element to our definition. Wisdom is:

- Extremely rare. High IQs exist as a small percentage of any population (because that's how IQ is defined), but godly wisdom was found nowhere else in the world. It is supremely valuable.

The wisdom of the King of kings

In a whole host of ways, the author shows us that wisdom is a wonderful thing. It is a gift of God's grace, in line with his promises, more to be valued than prosperity (though it may bring prosperity), and enables right moral judgements to govern the living of real life.

The 'WHO AM I?' TOOL helped us see that the dominant line of application must be from Solomon to Christ. We can rejoice that *he* is the supremely wise King, who will govern his people with righteousness and justice. In him 'are hidden all the treasures of wisdom and knowledge' (Colossians 2:3). What a blessing this is to us, and what happiness it will bring us as we come under his rule!

But the wise king doesn't just rule wisely. He also longs for his people to be wise. That's the reason Solomon wrote Proverbs, Ecclesiastes and Song of Songs, known collectively (with Job) as the 'Wisdom literature'. Perhaps you could read that next after 1 – 2 Kings. Or maybe take a proverb to reflect on each day over breakfast:

> The fear of the LORD is the beginning of knowledge;
>   fools despise wisdom and instruction.
> (Proverbs 1:7)

The gold telephone

1 Kings 5 – 8

If ever there is a need for the STRUCTURE TOOL, it is when we are approaching a huge slab of Bible meat like this. One of my (Andrew's) heroes at church was a lady called Betty, who lived to ninety-seven years old, and had a fascinating life. As a teenager she learned how to wield a cleaver and a bone saw at a South London butcher's shop. Twenty years later, Betty and her husband were serving as missionaries in Jamaica, running residential children's camps. There was a smallholding on site, where the staff raised beef cattle. Before Betty's arrival, their approach to butchery was simply to cube the cows and make a stew; she persuaded them that a better approach might be to distinguish between shin and chateaubriand and treat them slightly differently!

As we look for the biblical joints and sinews along which to run our knife, we discover a giant *inclusio* (the technical term for when a similar phrase tops and tails a section):

> And so I intend to build a house for the name of the LORD my God, as the LORD said to David my father, 'Your son, whom I will set on your throne in your place, shall build the house for my name.'
> (1 Kings 5:5)

> Now the LORD has fulfilled his promise that he made. For I have risen in the place of David my father, and sit on the throne of Israel, as the LORD promised, and I have built the house for the name of the LORD, the God of Israel.
> (1 Kings 8:20)

That suggests that 5:1 – 8:21 belongs together, giving us two sections:

5:1 – 8:21   Building the Temple
8:22–66   Dedicating the Temple

However, Dale Ralph Davis suggests a different structure for chapter 8:[1]

verses 1–13   Celebration and sacrifice
verses 14–21   Blessing Israel and the LORD
verses 22–53   Solomon's prayer of dedication
verses 54–61   Blessing Israel and the LORD
verses 62–6   Celebration and sacrifice

You have to be a bit wary of neat-looking structures in commentaries, which aren't always as clear when you try to find them in the text! But Professor Davis is a faithful guide, and his structure is also backed up by *inclusios*:

> The king ... blessed all the assembly of Israel ... And he said, 'Blessed be the LORD ...'
> (1 Kings 8:14–15)

> [Solomon] blessed all the assembly of Israel ... saying, 'Blessed be the LORD ...'
> (1 Kings 8:55–6)

Now we're in a pickle. Do we keep chapter 8 together (Davis) or break it at verse 22 (us)? There are good reasons to read the arrival of the ark as the climax of the building project (us). But it's also helpful to see that the central prayer of dedication is framed by the praises and sacrifices to a promise-keeping God (Davis). In this

---

1 Dale Ralph Davis, *The Wisdom and the Folly: An exposition of the book of First Kings* (Fearn: Christian Focus, 2002), p. 80.

case maybe we can have our steak and eat it. There are overlapping structures in Scripture, just as French and English butchers have different ways of slicing a cow.[2]

Building the Temple (1 Kings 5:1 – 8:21)

Beware of skipping over all the details of the Temple construction and its furnishing. There is a reason why the divinely inspired author decided to spend four chapters on it: he wants to impress upon us the weight of its glory. There were no video cameras or *National Geographic* documentaries in those days, and even if there had been, an accredited press pass wouldn't have got you anywhere near the Holy of Holies. But with the power of words, we are given a glimpse inside.

If we understand Temple doctrine but remain unmoved by its grandeur, then something is amiss.

> **Dig deeper exercise**
>
> Use the TONE AND FEEL TOOL as you consider how the author conveys the glory of the Temple.
> - The quality of the building materials (REPETITION TOOL: 'gold').
> - The scale of things – how many animals, how many labourers, how many cubits high?
> - The intricacy of the craftsmanship (if you don't know how beautiful a pomegranate is in cross-section, now is the time to head to a greengrocer!).
> - The hushed reverence with which the building work is undertaken (6:7).

By way of analogy, we thought of the effect of visiting a building like St Paul's Cathedral or York Minster. People naturally fall silent,

---

2 See *Larousse Gastronomique* (English ed., London: Hamlyn, 2009) at pages 83–4, which shows, for example, that a British butcher would slice the bit of beef at the rear of a cow into topside and thick flank, whereas a Frenchman would place his knife somewhere different to divide it into the *gîte à la noix* and the *romsteck*. It's gratifying that the authoritative French guide to cookery grants British butchery as a *possible* approach.

and not only because of the austere notices instructing you to do so! As the poet Hugh Chesterman wrote of the architect of St Paul's:

> Clever men like Christopher Wren
> Only occur just now and then.
> No one expects in perpetuity
> Architects of his ingenuity;
> No, never a cleverer dipped his pen
> Than clever Sir Christopher – Christopher Wren.[3]

And yet, we might say, the architect of the Temple makes Sir Christopher look like a novice and makes St Paul's look like it was cobbled together on the cheap.

The Temple was also of unique theological significance (unlike cathedrals, beautiful though they are). We see several key themes come together:

- *God's promises*. In 5:5 and 8:20 (the *inclusio* we noticed above), the trigger for the Temple-building project is Solomon's awareness of God's promises to David back in 2 Samuel 7, which he quotes verbatim (QUOTATION/ALLUSION TOOL). God's promise of a 'house' (dynasty for David) and of a 'house' (Temple) were inextricably linked.
- *Wisdom*. We are told twice (REPETITION TOOL, 5:7, 12) that Solomon's actions showcase his wisdom. If we zoom out and use the STRUCTURE TOOL, we discover that descriptions of Solomon's wisdom bracket the whole Temple narrative.

4:29–34	People of all nations came to hear Solomon's wisdom
5:1–18	Account of Hiram's assistance and the use of forced labour
6:1 – 9:9	Temple

---

[3] 'A poem from the tercentenary of Wren's death on 1923 by Hugh Chesterman': highamhall.com/wp-content/uploads/2020/05/A-poem-from-the-tercentenary-of-Wren.pdf (accessed 26 July 2024).

1 Kings 5 – 8

9:10–28 Account of Hiram's assistance and the use of forced labour

10:1–13 Queen of Sheba comes to hear Solomon's wisdom

- *Gathering of the nations.* Our attention is drawn to the contributions of two men, both called Hiram (obviously a popular boy's name at the time), who are from Tyre (5:1, 7:13) – in other words, foreigners! This is the first hint of a theme that grows in importance as we trace it through this section (8:41–3, 60) and throughout Scripture (e.g., Isaiah 2:1–11; Ephesians 2:11–22).
- *Redemption.* The author of 1 – 2 Kings repeatedly reminds us of how God rescued his people 'out of the land of Egypt' (REPETITION TOOL 6:1; 8:9, 16, 21). These multiple allusions to the exodus underline that God's dwelling with his people is only possible because of his past work of redemption. Moreover, the completion of the Temple is narrated in almost exactly the same terms (QUOTATION/ALLUSION TOOL) as the completion of the tabernacle in the book of Exodus (see Table 3).

Then the cloud covered the tent of meeting, and the glory of the LORD filled the tabernacle. And Moses was not able to enter the tent of meeting because the cloud settled on it, and the glory of the LORD filled the tabernacle. (Exodus 40:34–5)	And when the priests came out of the Holy Place, a cloud filled the house of the LORD, so that the priests could not stand to minister because of the cloud, for the glory of the LORD filled the house of the LORD. (1 Kings 8:10–11)

Table 3 **Glory!**

We can summarise all of this in a diagram (see Figure 6).

Ideally this diagram should be in gold leaf (a suggestion sadly vetoed by our publisher). The glory of the physical structure combined with the glory of its theological significance is meant to leave us awestruck and full of praise.

The gold telephone

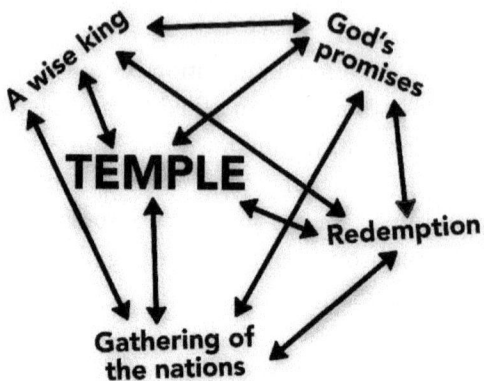

Figure 6 **The Temple at the heart of everything**

Dedicating the Temple (1 Kings 8:22–66)

The best questions in a small group Bible study are those without an easy yes or no answer, the ones that make you really think hard. How about this one: did God live in the Temple or not?

You might want to answer 'yes' on the basis of verse 11 – the cloud of God's glory has come to fill the Temple. Or you might say 'no' because in verse 27 Solomon recognises that God cannot be contained by heaven itself, let alone fitted into this tiny man-made structure. On the basis of a similar passage in Isaiah 66:1–2, Stephen rebuked the Jewish leaders who had later come to idolise the Temple: 'the Most High does not dwell in houses made by hands' (Acts 7:48). The Apostle Paul told the Athenians the same (Acts 17:24).

OK, so it's definitely a 'no', then? Hmm. But there's surely *something* very special about this place, because in verse 29 God says, 'My name shall be there.' On the other hand, his 'dwelling place' is not here but 'in heaven' (verse 30). The tension is surely deliberate. Theologians speak in terms of God's *transcendence* and his *immanence*:

'To say that God is transcendent is to say that he is exalted, above, beyond us. To say that God is immanent is to say that he is present in time and space, that he is near us.'[4]

The Temple plays a crucial role in bridging the gap between God and us. We instinctively think of it as the place of sacrifice, remembering perhaps the Day of Atonement ceremonies focused on its predecessor the tabernacle, but the emphasis here is on the Temple's role as a *communication channel*.[5]

As an illustration, the Temple is functioning a little like a telephone box. God doesn't live there, but there is a hotline to him (or more accurately, it is like a telephone *exchange*, because you don't have to physically be at the Temple, but merely to pray towards it – in the same way that Muslims pray towards Mecca, Mohammed presumably having derived the idea from Judaism). We easily miss the significance, because we are so accustomed to the new covenant privilege of access to God and his forgiveness any time, anywhere (we've upgraded to spiritual smartphones). But at this stage in Bible history, the Temple provides a level of access that God's people haven't enjoyed before.

The author captures this idea with a vivid and unforgettable metaphor in verse 29, where he asks God that 'your eyes may be open … that you may listen'! The same turn of phrase crops up in verse 52, at the end of the prayer. It's not that Solomon is confused about the role of different sensory organs. He's just asking God to pay attention, to maintain eye contact as it were, not to turn his face away.

If the Temple is a telephone exchange, what is the subject of most of the calls diverted through it? 'God … is that you? … I'm sorry. Please forgive me' (verse 30).

---

[4] John M. Frame, 'Divine Transcendence and Immanence', The Gospel Coalition: www.thegospelcoalition.org/essay/divine-transcendence-immanence (accessed 29 July 2024). The whole article is worth reading, as is, in our experience, anything written by John Frame.

[5] Interestingly, when the New Testament wants to make a point about atonement, it often refers to the tabernacle rather than the Temple (e.g., Hebrews 8 – 10; Romans 3:25 – the word *hilastērion* translates as the 'mercy seat'). Whereas the Temple primarily signifies a place of communion with God/prayer.

Solomon

Communication is essential to mending a broken relationship. Maybe you've been in the situation where someone is so angry with you that when you call to say sorry they don't pick up. The phone just rings and rings. Or worse, they block your number.

Solomon is scared that the same thing might happen with God, so he asks seven times that when the people pray in or towards the Temple God would 'hear in heaven' (REPETITION TOOL, verses 32, 34, 36, 39, 43, 45, 49) and in most cases the request is that he would 'forgive' (REPETITION TOOL, verses 34, 36, 39, 50).

The QUOTATION/ALLUSION TOOL reveals that many of Solomon's requests are based on the covenant curses that God has threatened to bring on Israel if they disobey (see Table 4).

As we read on, we will discover that they end up praying exactly these prayers in exactly these situations. There will be military defeat (15:20). There will be drought (17:1; 18:1). Finally and tragically, there will be exile (2 Kings 17:6; 24:10–17). Isn't it remarkable that Solomon *anticipates* all of this? Well, not really. He is wise. He knows what God said in the law of Moses. And he knows the wickedness of the human heart: 'If they sin against you – for there is no one who does not sin' (8:46).

Verses	Situation	Covenantal curse?
31–2	One man sinning against his neighbour	
33–4	Military defeat on account of the people's sin	Leviticus 26:17 Deuteronomy 28:25
35–6	Shutting up of the heavens and lack of rain on account of the people's sin	Leviticus 26:19–20 Deuteronomy 28:23–4
37–40	Any conceivable type of disaster, personal or national (the catch-all clause!)	Leviticus 26:25 Deuteronomy 28:21–2, 38–9, 42
41–3	A foreigner seeks help from God	
44–5	Military threat	
46–51	Exile on account of the people's sin	Leviticus 26:33 Deuteronomy 28:36–7, 41, 49–50, 64–8

Table 4 **Prayers in anticipation of various covenant curses**

Did you notice where the pray-er is located? At first Solomon imagines him 'before your altar in this house' (verse 31), then simply 'in this house' (verse 33), then far away but praying 'towards this house' (verses 35, 38, 42), then 'towards this city' (verse 44), and then even further, in exile, praying 'towards their land' (verse 48; remember how Daniel prayed 'towards Jerusalem', Daniel 6:10). To continue our telecoms analogy, this is like testing the range of a mobile phone as it moves further and further from the antenna. Solomon knows that sin can and will create huge distances between people and God. So he petitions God to hear them even when they have strayed very far.

Even as he asks God to hear his people's cries for mercy, Solomon is keen that easy access to forgiveness shouldn't encourage casual disobedience.[6] So he concludes with both a prayer and an exhortation: the people are told to obey, and God is asked to move them to obey. The PARALLELS TOOL shows us how tightly verses 58 and 61 are aligned:

> 'May [he] incline our hearts to him, to walk in all his ways and keep his commandments, his statutes, and his rules, which he commanded our fathers' (verse 58).

> 'Let your heart ... be wholly true to the LORD our God, walking in his statutes and keeping his commandments...' (verse 61).

Praying in Jesus' name

The Temple displayed God's glory and provided a much-needed communication channel with God, by which his people might ask for forgiveness when they sinned.

In the New Testament, the Temple finds fulfilment in three ways: Jesus is the temple (e.g., John 2:21; Revelation 21:22); Christians are temples (1 Corinthians 6:19), and the gathered assembly of

---

6 Just as Jude warns of those who 'pervert the grace of God into sensuality' (Jude 4).

believers is a temple (Ephesians 2:21–2). The fulfilment in Jesus is primary because it underpins the other two; we are 'built up as a spiritual house' only as we 'come to him' (1 Peter 2:4–5).

If we replace 'TEMPLE' in Figure 6 with 'JESUS,' and use even more gold leaf, then we can appreciate how the same cluster of theological truths finds its fulfilment in him. He is the truly wise King, who brings God's promises to fulfilment in a new act of redemption that encompasses even Gentiles. Let us rejoice in him.

We often focus on Jesus' fulfilment of the *sacrificial* function of the Temple but neglect the fact that he also opened up a channel of *communication* with God. Without Jesus as our temple, our prayers for mercy could not reach heaven. But because of him, when we pray 'in Jesus' name', God hears us and forgives us, even when we have strayed a long way and want to come home. And he gives us a fresh desire to obey him.

1 Kings 8 is a great resource to fuel those prayers; verses 46–53 in particular provide one of the most beautiful confessions in Scripture. Why not incorporate it in your personal prayers this week?

> If they sin against you – for there is no one who does not sin – and you are angry with them and give them to an enemy, so that they are carried away captive to the land of the enemy, far off or near, yet if they turn their heart in the land to which they have been carried captive, and repent and plead with you in the land of their captors, saying, 'We have sinned and have acted perversely and wickedly', if they repent with all their mind and with all their heart in the land of their enemies, who carried them captive, and pray to you towards their land, which you gave to their fathers, the city that you have chosen, and the house that I have built for your name, then hear in heaven your dwelling place their prayer and their plea, and maintain their cause and forgive your people who have sinned against you, and all their transgressions that they have committed against you, and grant them compassion in the sight of those who carried them captive, that they may

have compassion on them (for they are your people, and your heritage, which you brought out of Egypt, from the midst of the iron furnace). Let your eyes be open to the plea of your servant and to the plea of your people Israel, giving ear to them whenever they call to you. For you separated them from among all the peoples of the earth to be your heritage, as you declared through Moses your servant, when you brought our fathers out of Egypt, O Lord God.
(1 Kings 8:46–53)

It took her breath away

1 Kings 9 – 10

The story is told of a couple with two sons. One son was an optimist and the other a pessimist. One Christmas, bemused by the differences between their children, Mum and Dad decided to conduct an experiment. They snuck in during the night and filled the pessimist's bedroom with toys piled to the ceiling. Meanwhile for the optimist they left a note in his room, 'You'll find your present in the garage,' where they had had delivered a cartload of horse manure.

The next morning they awoke to wailing from the pessimist's room. 'All these lovely toys,' he said, tears streaming down his face. 'I'll never have time to play with all of them!' At this point they were interrupted by a whoop of joy from the garage. They went down to find their other son digging around in the manure, beaming. 'All this dung,' he said, 'there's got to be a pony in here somewhere!'

This time we are not going to take the passage section by section in the usual way. Rather, we'll work through the whole thing twice, first enjoying the good news of God blessing Solomon's kingdom, and second noting undertones of growing unease. Our fear was, if we dealt with the two themes together – blessing mixed with unease – the pessimists among you would let the unease take over and you would feel nothing of the blessing!

The happy read-through

The first of God's blessings in this section is the answer 'Yes' to Solomon's prayer. He asked that God's 'eyes may be open … that

1 Kings 9 – 10

you may listen' (CONTEXT TOOL 8:29), and God now replies that his 'eyes and [his] heart will be there for all time' (9:3), a reassurance that the people's prayers for forgiveness will be heard. Amazing!

After a discussion of the logistics of the Temple-building project, we are told about Solomon's sea-faring expeditions and extraordinary income from trade; a single expedition brings in 14 tonnes of gold (9:26–8; 10:22). Given that all the gold ever mined is still somewhere in circulation, it's a fun thought that some of your wedding ring might once have belonged to him.

The blessings reach a crescendo with the 'Arrival of the Queen of Sheba' (we suggest you type this into Spotify and listen to Handel's soundtrack as you read – we have it on loop as we write). There's lots that impresses her, but the REPETITION TOOL quickly reveals the author's emphasis. When the Queen sets Solomon a difficult exam and he passes it with 100%, she testifies to 'all the *wisdom* of Solomon' (verses 1–4). She has heard before of his 'words and [his] *wisdom*' (verse 6), but now sees for herself his '*wisdom* and prosperity' (verse 7). How happy are his servants, she comments, to be able to hear his '*wisdom*' (verse 8).

Then we learn that the Queen of Sheba's visit was not a one-off, but one state visit among many. The 'whole earth' came to seek Solomon's God-given wisdom, and 'every one of them' brought lavish gifts to him 'year by year' (10:23–5).

If we zoom out and take a panoramic view of 1 Kings so far, we realise we have seen several of these themes already.

Previously: God answers Solomon's prayer for wisdom at Gibeon (3:10–14).
Now: God answers Solomon's prayer for the Temple, appearing 'a second time, as … at Gibeon' (9:1–3).

Previously: 'Judah and Israel … were happy' (4:20).
Now: 'Happy are your men! Happy are your servants' (10:8).

Previously: 'People of all nations came to hear the wisdom of Solomon' (4:34).

Now: 'The whole earth sought the presence of Solomon to hear his wisdom' (10:24).

God's kingdom flourishes under a wise king and his people experience great blessing. Solomon's wisdom was so notable that even when we want to express amazement nowadays, we often do so using phrases borrowed from chapter 10: 'It took my breath away' (verse 5), 'I wasn't told the half of it' (verse 7) or, 'I had to see it with my own eyes' (verse 7)!

> **Dig deeper exercise**
> We saw in 1 Kings 3 – 4 that the 'who am i?' tool helps us to avoid the trap of the Prosperity Gospel. Solomon was rich beyond our wildest dreams. That does not mean we will be rich beyond our wildest dreams.
> Read 10:8–9.
> Solomon is the rich and glorious king, but who is happy (verse 8)?
> Solomon is the just and righteous king, but to whom has God shown love by crowning him (verse 9)?
> The equivalent of Solomon for a New Testament believer is _____ (there's a further clue in Matthew 12:42 if you're not sure).
> The people who benefit from his riches and rule are _____.
> The people to whom God has shown love by crowning him are _____.

In the Lord's Prayer, we pray, 'Your kingdom come,' and often have little sense of what we are asking for, or what that would look like. The days of Solomon give us a concrete example in history. It looks like prosperity, security, justice and happiness. It looks like God hearing your prayers. It looks like all the nations bringing their tribute and laying it at the feet of God's king.

The read-through of growing unease

We have noted already that the success of Solomon's dynasty is contingent on the king's obedience (CONTEXT TOOL 2:2–4; see also 3:14; 6:11–13). This time it's different, because the negative consequences of *dis*obedience are spelled out for the first time (9:6–9). We discover that the very blessings the people are enjoying are under threat (see Table 5).

Current blessing	Threat in case of disobedience
Prosperity in the land	'I will cut off Israel from the land' (verse 7).
International fame	'Israel will become a proverb and a byword among all peoples' (verse 7).
A temple where God put his name, and where his eyes will be	'The house that I have consecrated for my name I will cast out of my sight' (verse 7). It will 'become a heap of ruins' (verse 8).

Table 5 **Blessings and threats**

The other new thing is that God specifies the sin that will cause this ruin: 'if you … go and serve other gods and worship them' (verse 6) and 'because they … laid hold on other gods and worshipped them and served them' (verse 9). This reminder not to break the first of the Ten Commandments sets the stage for the tragedy about to unfold.

This first note of unease having been sounded so loudly, we start to notice other more subtle melodies in a minor key. Hiram, previously a prime example of Solomon's wise international relations, now seems disgruntled at his apparent mistreatment (9:12–14).

Second, the author tells us that Solomon's draft of forced labour was drawn from those 'whom the people of Israel were unable to devote to destruction' (9:21, NARRATOR'S COMMENT TOOL). To fully appreciate the significance of this, we need to revise the backstory:

- God commanded the destruction of the Canaanites in Deuteronomy 20:17–18.

- The Israelites disobeyed, instead putting them to forced labour (Judges 1:28, 30, 33, 35).
- God warned that, as a result, the Canaanites 'shall become thorns in your sides and their gods shall be a snare to you' (Judges 2:3).

Finally, although Solomon's vast personal gold reserves (10:14–21) and large number of horses (10:26), sourced partly from Egypt (10:28), seem on first reading to be something to celebrate, when played alongside Deuteronomy 17:16–17 the harmonies begin to jar:

> He [Israel's king] must not acquire many horses for himself or cause the people to return to Egypt in order to acquire many horses, since the LORD has said to you, 'You shall never return that way again.' And he shall not acquire many wives for himself, lest his heart turn away, nor shall he acquire for himself excessive silver and gold.

Too good to be true?

What is the author's intention in weaving these undertones of unease throughout what is otherwise a symphony of joy? Surely to show us that all we are celebrating is precarious. Israel at this point in history enjoys great blessing, but it is not entirely secure. As a result, the reader is unable to relax. It's a bit like watching the first five minutes of an episode of *Casualty* (the UK's longest-running hospital drama of all time): the camera shows nothing but happy images – giggling children, laughing mothers, a smiling crane operator lowering a huge girder – but all the viewer can think of is the impending visit to A&E.

The situation of the Christian is wonderfully different. We have a King who will never fail and are receiving a kingdom that cannot be shaken. Jesus never turned aside from his Father's commandments. He dealt generously with every 'Hiram' who came across his path. He was not willing to compromise with God's enemies.

He didn't seek excessive gold for himself; indeed, 'though he was rich, yet for [our] sake he became poor, so that [we] by his poverty might become rich' (2 Corinthians 8:9). Consequently, the kingdom is safe in his hands. Nothing can threaten our happiness or the enjoyment of God's blessing that is grounded in him.

Trouble and strife x700
1 Kings 11:1–25

Chocolate bar manufacturers indicate, using little grooves, how much (they think!) you should eat in one go. In the same way, biblical authors indicate the breaks between sections using a variety of 'grooves'. (The editors of our modern Bibles also make decisions about where to put paragraph breaks, subheadings, etc., but they aren't infallible, and it's good practice to try to ignore their divisions as you do the detective work for yourself.) Sometimes there's a change of scene or subject matter. Here, there is a change of protagonist. Solomon is the subject of almost every verb in verses 1–8. From verse 9 onwards, the LORD becomes the subject. And so it breaks up into the following mouthfuls:

11:1-8   Solomon's heart turns away from the LORD.
11:9-13   The LORD pronounces judgement (with mercy).
11:14-25 The LORD executes judgement – Hadad and Rezon.

It's a bar of chocolate that leaves a very bitter taste.

The domino effect (1 Kings 11:1–8)

There is a best-selling self-improvement book called *The Seven Habits of Highly Effective People*, but we much prefer the spoof, *The 77 Habits of Highly Ineffective Christians*.[1] It has chapters like 'Embrace the triangle of mediocrity' (which comprises the TV, the remote control and the couch). Of course, the point of the book

---

[1] Chris Fabry, *The 77 Habits of Highly Ineffective Christians* (Leicester: Crossway Books, 1997).

is actually to tell you how to be effective in your discipleship, by showing what the opposite looks like (C. S. Lewis famously did something similar with *The Screwtape Letters*).

In the same spirit we offer you some advice, drawn from 1 Kings 11, on how to fall away. Just follow these simple steps and you'll be guaranteed to shipwreck your faith.

Step one: ignore the warnings about a 'lesser' sin

Solomon's sin has two parts to it: he marries foreign women and he worships foreign gods. God's law warned him that the two sins go together like a pair of adjacent dominos: when the first falls, the second will inexorably follow: 'surely they will turn away your heart after their gods' (verse 2).[2]

But Solomon doesn't heed the warning. Doubtless Chemosh-worship appalled him to begin with, and he wasn't even remotely tempted by it. But what would be the harm in a date with that beautiful girl from Moab? Love is always a good thing, right?

It's true that marrying someone is not as bad as bowing down to a false god. But what if one thing leads to the other? Solomon thinks it won't. God said it will. Has God exaggerated the consequences because he's a spoilsport? It sounds like the Fall of Adam and Eve all over again (Genesis 3:1–6).

For us, one of the most chilling details in the story comes in verse 4: it is only when he is 'old' that the consequences kick in. He gets married once and nothing happens. He finds himself still worshipping God. So he gets married a second time. Again, no thunderbolt from heaven. No burning desire to construct an altar to Milcom. So why not plan a third wedding? And a fourth?

Solomon reigns for forty years (11:42), and gets married in total seven hundred times, which if the weddings were evenly spaced would be one every three weeks! You can imagine him phoning the florist on speed dial. 'Hi, it's me; the usual please.' An eye-watering

---

[2] The QUOTATION/ALLUSION TOOL reminds us to consult the original context of a quotation, and verse 2 sends us back to Deuteronomy 7:1–4 or Exodus 34:11–16.

number of weddings. Zero false gods worshipped. He's got away with it.

Step two: wait

We've called it step two, but really Solomon doesn't need to do anything else. Once you've toppled the first domino in a domino run, you don't need to push the second one over. As the REPETITION TOOL shows us, that takes care of itself:

> 'Surely they will turn away your heart after their gods' (verse 2).
> His wives turned away his heart (verse 3).
> His wives turned away his heart after other gods (verse 4).
> His heart had turned away from the LORD (verse 9).

The CONTEXT TOOL makes us feel the tragedy more keenly. First, because this comes hot on the heels of ten chapters celebrating the glorious high point of the kingdom of Israel. There's nowhere else in Bible history that gets as close to a foretaste of the new creation. However, we've seen that all of these blessings are conditional on the king's obedience (1 Kings 2:3-4; 6:11-13; 9:4-9), and now the whole thing is poised on the brink of disaster.

The TONE AND FEEL TOOL reminds us to pause on the details in verses 5-8. Why does the author list all the specific gods? He does it so that he can say the word 'abomination' three times; so that he can horrify us with the mention of Molech, the god who demanded child sacrifice (see Leviticus 20:1-9); so that he can drum home that Solomon was *colossally wrong*, and that the consequences came, and they were terrible.

> **Dig deeper exercise**
>
> Use the LINKING WORDS TOOL. How do verses 9-13 follow from what Solomon has done? Look out for words like 'because' and 'since'.
> Why is this cause-and-effect relationship essential to understanding God's anger?

Judgement pronounced (1 Kings 11:9–13)

The LORD is angry with Solomon. The author slows things so that we feel the rightness of God's indignation. God has appeared to Solomon 'twice' (verse 9). To reject him after such gracious revelation is a real kick in the teeth. Moreover, God has 'commanded him concerning this thing, that he should not go after other gods', yet that is precisely what he does.

Then God assumes the role of judge as he sums up the crime (verse 11a) and pronounces sentence (verse 11b). The vivid language of 'tearing' the kingdom away will return in the next chapter in the context of Ahijah's prophecy. Yet 'for the sake of David' (REPETITION TOOL verses 12, 13, 32, 34), judgement is tempered with mercy. This must be a reference back to the promise that God made to David in 2 Samuel 7:14–15 that, even if his son should sin, 'my steadfast love will not depart from him'. Like the First World War song, 'Keep the Home Fires Burning', or The Smiths' 1980s classic, 'There's a Light that Never Goes Out', or Tolkien's Silmarils (Andrew, being less of a *Lord of the Rings* geek than Alasdair, doesn't get this one), this thread of undying hope is described as an unextinguished flame: 'David my servant may always have a lamp before me in Jerusalem' (verse 36).

We've mentioned before a tension between the seeming unconditionality of that promise and the conditional warnings that run through 1 Kings. Here that tension is at its fullest stretch. Solomon's sin demands judgement but God's promises demand mercy.

We are told that God's mercy is also 'for the sake of Jerusalem' (verse 13). This is because Jerusalem is home to the Temple, the place where God had promised to hear prayers for forgiveness. Forgiveness is so desperately needed now.

Judgement carried out (1 Kings 11:14–25)

We read that the LORD twice 'raised up an adversary' (verses 14, 23) against Solomon. God begins to execute the sentence he has pronounced.

Solomon

Like Janus, the Roman false god (it seemed an appropriate illustration) who faces both forwards and back, the CONTEXT TOOL will help us in both directions:

- Looking back (taking up our cue from verses 15–16 and 24), we are reminded that David had defeated both the Edomites and a king called Hadadezer, in 2 Samuel 8:3–13. Now their respective successors are back to exact revenge. Is there further significance in the fact that David's victory came immediately after the *making* of the covenant in 2 Samuel 7, but it turns sour and comes back to bite Solomon immediately after the *breaking* of the covenant in 1 Kings 11:1–8?
- Looking back, we are invited again to reflect on the Exodus story. Previously, we saw that the dedication of the Temple was linked to the completion of the tabernacle, when God had brought them 'out of Egypt' (1 Kings 8:9, 16, 21, 53). Then we began to feel uneasy as Solomon resembled Pharaoh in the way he drafted slaves (9:21) and amassed chariots and horses from Egypt (10:26–9). Now, in judgement on Solomon, Hadad becomes a kind of anti-Moses: he goes to Egypt (11:17), is taken into Pharaoh's house (verses 19–20) and says the equivalent of 'let my people go' (verses 21–2, the same verb in Hebrew as Exodus 7:16, etc.).[3]
- Looking forward, we shall discover that some of the details we are told about the two adversaries Hadad and Rezon deliberately foreshadow the life of Jeroboam, the anti-hero of the next section. He too 'fled from his master' (verse 40; compare verse 23) and he too receives help from Pharaoh (verse 40; compare verse 19). We therefore infer that Jeroboam, like Hadad and Rezon, is an adversary raised up by God in consequence of Solomon's sin.

---

3 Peter J. Leithart, *1 & 2 Kings* (Grand Rapids, MI: Brazos Press, 2006), p. 87.

Solomon, Jesus and me

As the heart of the king turns away from God, so the kingdom is torn apart. Because the fate of the people is bound up with the fate of the king, the whole nation suffers. The golden age of peace and prosperity is over.

The 'WHO AM I?' TOOL reminds us not to jump immediately into Solomon's shoes. The primary line of application is always from the king of Israel to Jesus, in this case by way of contrast. Unlike Solomon, Jesus never doubted his Father's words and consequently his heart never turned away. Thus his kingdom is secure, and he reigns over a united people.

But in this case, we can learn a direct lesson from Solomon also. The prohibition on marrying unbelievers in Deuteronomy 7:1–4 and Exodus 34:11–16 was not specific to the king. What he did wrong would have been wrong for any Israelite. For this reason, Nehemiah used him as an object lesson for those believers in his own day who had married pagans:

> In those days also I saw the Jews who had married women of Ashdod, Ammon, and Moab. And half of their children spoke the language of Ashdod, and they could not speak the language of Judah, but only the language of each people. And I confronted them and cursed them and beat some of them and pulled out their hair. And I made them swear in the name of God, saying, 'You shall not give your daughters to their sons, or take their daughters for your sons or for yourselves. Did not Solomon king of Israel sin on account of such women? Among the many nations there was no king like him, and he was beloved by his God, and God made him king over all Israel. Nevertheless, foreign women made even him to sin. Shall we then listen to you and do all this great evil and act treacherously against our God by marrying foreign women?'
> (Nehemiah 13:23–7)

After all, inappropriate relationships are so frequently the cause of Christians turning away from God. No one plans this, and all intend to keep the second domino standing. We just think God is bluffing when he warns us that the first domino stands close enough to topple it. 'Marrying the nice Hindu girl or dating the charming atheist boy isn't the worst sin,' says someone. 'He said he might even come to church with me sometimes,' says another. 'I know she worships Molech, but she admired my Temple too,' said Solomon. And we've seen where it ended up.

Of course, there will be some readers who are painfully conscious of having married unwisely. The Bible is clear that once you have tied the knot, in most cases (the exceptions being adultery and abuse) you should remain together, even if your spouse is an unbeliever. And God's grace is sufficient for all our past failings. People in this situation must take care, with God's help, to keep the second domino standing, as the first leans heavily against it.

But to the reader who is not yet married, we urge you to heed the warning of Solomon, the wisest man in history who became the most foolish of all.

THE
DIVIDED
KINGDOM

1 Kings 11:26 – 12:24
1 Kings 11:26 – 12:24

Marilynne Robinson is a Christian writer, and a sneaky lady. In a volume of essays called *The Death of Adam* she includes one entitled 'Marguerite de Navarre' that begins like this:

> The title of this essay is somewhat misleading. My intention, my hope, is to revive interest in Jean Cauvin, the sixteenth-century French humanist and theologian ... known to us as John Calvin. If I had been forthright about my subject, I doubt that the average reader would have read this far ... People know to disapprove of him, though not precisely why they should ...[1]

The rest of the chapter is entirely about Calvin. The *next* chapter is called 'Marguerite de Navarre: Part II' and is actually about Marguerite de Navarre!

Marilynne Robinson knew that the doctrine particularly associated with Calvin – the idea that God chooses who is saved and predestines our future – has such a bad press, even among some Christians, that her only hope of getting a hearing was to disguise the title of her essay.

We want to talk about Calvinism in this chapter. But we are not calling it 'Calvinism', still less naming it after a sixteenth-century French noblewoman. We are calling it '1 Kings 11:26 – 12:24'. Because the fact is, Calvin didn't invent Calvinism. He got it

---
1 Marilynne Robinson, *The Death of Adam: Essays on modern thought* (New York, NY: Picador, 1998), p. 174.

straight from Jesus (e.g., John 6:44; 15:16) or the Apostle Paul (e.g., Ephesians 1:4–5) or the Apostle Peter (1 Peter 2:8b–9) or the book of Acts (13:48) or 1 Kings 11:26 – 12:24.

People struggle with God's sovereignty – his absolute control over everything in history, including human decisions – because they think it makes us robots. They are worried that everything we do would be the result of our programming rather than our personhood. They fear that it turns us into fatalists; we are not free; nothing is our fault.

The Bible never sees it like that. Again and again we find strong assertions of God's sovereignty side by side with strong assertions of our human choice and responsibility for our actions. Don't these contradict each other? Not according to Scripture. Not according to 1 Kings 11:26 – 12:24.

The Incredible Hulk prophet (11:26–43)

The story begins with a summary: 'Jeroboam the son of Nebat … lifted up his hand [i.e., he raised a fist] against the king' (verse 26). It's a story of rebellion, a civil war, a successful coup. It's introduced from the perspective of Jeroboam's freely chosen action.

But then we are told 'the reason why he lifted up his hand against the king' (verse 27) and it turns out to be a divine prophecy. It now appears that it was all God's idea! Does that mean Jeroboam had nothing to do with it? Of course not. God's sovereignty and Jeroboam's responsibility are 'both–and', not 'either–or'.

Jeroboam, a high-flyer on Solomon's civil service fast track (verse 28), is going about his business one day when he meets the prophet Ahijah who, he can't help noticing, is wearing a rather flash new suit (verse 29). Without warning, Ahijah violently shreds his jacket into twelve pieces (Andrew winces at the memory of his attempt to replicate this while preaching on 1 Kings 11 and how the congregation watched patiently as he tried in vain to get the shirt to rip). Ahijah then announces the tearing-up of the kingdom and its division between Solomon's son and Jeroboam in a ratio of ten tribes to one (verse 31).

The mathematically astute reader will spot that ten plus one doesn't quite add up to twelve, but probably the idea is that Solomon's son automatically keeps his own tribe (Judah) and then gets 'one' extra – most likely Benjamin because of the way the battle lines are drawn in 12:21-3. But the maths is less the focus than the tragedy.

And all of it is because of Solomon's sin. In fact, had we been a bit stricter with the STRUCTURE TOOL, we would have included this as part of the Solomon story – the author doesn't sign off on him with the standard royal reign summary until 11:41-3.

Most of Ahijah's message is given over to telling us, once more for good measure, the lessons we've already learned about Solomon's idolatry and God's mercy:

- Solomon's crime is stated again in verse 33, albeit with an interesting shift in pronoun: God will tear away the kingdom 'because *they* have ...' The plural highlights the way that the king's sin infects his subjects. We shall see this theme again and again in 1 – 2 Kings.

- God's mercy is mentioned again many times, on account of his promise to David (REPETITION TOOL verses 32, 34, 36) and for the sake of the prayers heard in the Temple in Jerusalem (REPETITION TOOL verses 32, 36).

But let's get back to our Calvinism controversy. God prophesied the tearing and Jeroboam lifted up his hand. They go together. At this stage there doesn't seem any mystery involved. Jeroboam simply responds to what God says. It's about to get a little more complicated ...

Angry young men (1 Kings 12:1–14)

The next scene in our narrative is all about a human decision. One of Rehoboam's first tasks as the new king is to work out how to respond to their demands for a tax cut (verse 4).

The divided kingdom

First, he calls in the elder statesmen who had 'stood before Solomon his father' (verse 6) – not a bad choice, given that those who used to 'continually stand before [Solomon] and hear [his] wisdom' (CONTEXT TOOL 10:8) were the envy of the world. These world-class counsellors recommend that he should be a servant to his people, who would then gladly serve him (verse 7). Jesus would later give the same advice: 'Whoever would be great among you must be your servant, and whoever would be first among you must be slave of all.' Wonderfully, he lived and died by this standard (Mark 10:43–5).

But Rehoboam 'abandoned' this counsel and instead turned to his mates. The youngsters, with power going to their heads, drafted a somewhat different state of the kingdom speech: 'My little finger is thicker than my father's thighs' (verse 10). We won't spell it out for you, but let's just say the word 'finger' isn't in the original Hebrew; the sentiment might be a bit ruder than your English translation suggests.

'I'll be a strong leader,' Rehoboam thinks to himself. 'Compassion is for wimps.' And so he 'answered the people harshly' (verse 13).

Evidently, he hadn't spent much time reading the book that his father had specifically dedicated to him:

A soft answer turns away wrath,
   but a harsh word stirs up anger.
(Proverbs 15:1)

Without counsel plans fail,
   but with many advisers they succeed.
(Proverbs 15:22)

Sweetness of speech increases persuasiveness.
(Proverbs 16:21)

Plans are established by counsel;
   by wise guidance wage war.
(Proverbs 20:18)

Divide and conquer? (1 Kings 12:15–24)

In verse 15 we read that God planned all of this to fulfil his word. So it was all God's idea! Does that mean Rehoboam had nothing to do with it? Of course not. God's sovereignty and Rehoboam's responsibility are 'both-and', not 'either-or'.

The oppressed masses have had enough of Rehoboam's harsh government, and of their own free will they make Jeroboam king in Israel (to the north), leaving Rehoboam in control of Judah (in the south). Rehoboam, still believing his own hype, chooses to marshal an army to recapture the north in a grandiose display of strength (verse 21). The country is headed for civil war. But God sends another prophet, telling them to lay down arms because 'this thing is from me' (verse 24).

When we take a step back and consider the prophecies of Ahijah and Shemaiah side by side, we discover something remarkable. Ahijah's words were rejected by Solomon, who even tried to kill Jeroboam in order to thwart them (11:40). Shemaiah's words were accepted by Rehoboam, who abandoned the reconquest of the north in order to obey them. Yet both words were fulfilled.

Both–and

Human decisions are real and we are responsible for them. Yet all decisions must in the end conform to God's plans.

It reminds us of Paul's message to the crowds in Pisidian Antioch, perhaps the ultimate 'both-and' verse: 'For those who live in Jerusalem and their rulers, because they did not recognize [Jesus] nor understand the utterances of the prophets, which are read every Sabbath, fulfilled them by condemning him' (Acts 13:27).

> **Dig deeper exercise**
> Use the 'SO WHAT?!' TOOL.
> Why is it important to know that Solomon and Rehoboam were genuinely responsible for their foolish actions? What would we lose if we spoke *only* in terms of God's purposes?

Why is it important to know that God was in control of Israel's history, with all of its ups and downs? What would we lose if we spoke *only* in terms of human decision-making?

Why is it important to know Judas, the Jewish authorities, Pilate and the people were genuinely responsible for crucifying Jesus? What would we lose if we spoke *only* in terms of God's purposes? Why is it important to know that God was in control of Jesus' death? What would we lose if we spoke *only* in terms of human decision-making?

The lion, the altar and the failed disguise

1 Kings 12:25 – 14:20

God doesn't go moo (1 Kings 12:25–33)

Jeroboam son of Nebat has a problem. Even though he finds himself king of the breakaway province up north, most of the critical national infrastructure is still centred on Jerusalem across the new border. Jerusalem is home to the Temple and, more problematically, the palace of his rival Rehoboam. If his citizens maintain their thrice-annual pilgrimages for the major festivals, the drumbeat of support for reunification will grow louder and his position will be threatened.

Politically, his strategy is sound (verses 26–7): he sets up two local religious hubs, one at Dan and one at Bethel, to rival Jerusalem. Theologically, however, it is disastrous.

> **Dig deeper exercise**
> Use the QUOTATION/ALLUSION TOOL. Compare 12:28 with Exodus 32:4 to discover where Jeroboam got his idea for:
> - the centrepiece for his shrines;
> - the liturgy.
>
> Consider the original context of Exodus 32. How does the decision to worship God by means of a calf idol work out for the Israelites?

The words 'golden calf' should have sent the same kind of shudder down the spine of an ancient Israelite as 'Auschwitz' would for a twenty-first-century German. Perhaps Jeroboam is so biblically illiterate that he doesn't remember how the story ended.

Certainly, the author thinks Jeroboam is culpable and spells out that the whole scheme takes place at his own wicked initiative: it is he who plans it ('Jeroboam said in his heart,' verse 26) and he who implements it ('he set ... he put', verse 29). Not content with this, he appoints his own priesthood (verse 31) and makes up his own festivals (verse 32) – what we might call the 'Clinton Cards sin'.[1] The summary in verse 33 brings it to a climax:

> He went up to the altar *that he had made* in Bethel on the fifteenth day in the eighth month, in the month *that he had devised* from his own heart. And *he instituted* a feast for the people of Israel and went up to the altar to make offerings.[2]

The impact of Jeroboam's idolatry will be enormous. Just as William I of England is always known as 'William the Conqueror', Jeroboam I of Israel is always hereafter called 'Jeroboam son of Nebat' who 'made Israel to sin' (1 Kings 16:26; 21:22; 22:52; 2 Kings 3:3; 10:29; 13:2, 11; 14:24; 15:9, 18, 24, 28; 17:21). His is the sin that leads others to sin, the kind of wrong for which Jesus warned the consequences would be so dire that your better option would be to have a millstone fastened around your neck and be drowned in the depth of the sea (Matthew 18:6).

God will destroy the fake religion (1 Kings 13:1 – 14:20)

There's a lot going on in this section – a paralysed hand, a lion with strangely diminished appetite, a remarkably ineffective disguise. If we treat each episode in isolation, we are apt to run into trouble, not least because the author refuses to answer many of our questions about the details. It's only when we zoom out to look at them together (STRUCTURE TOOL) that we discern a striking pattern.

---

1 For international readers: Clinton Cards is a retail chain in the UK that sells greetings cards for every well-known occasion ('Happy Birthday'; 'With Condolences') and for some rather less-well-known occasions ...

2 Emphasis added.

God speaks through three prophets in succession; each makes two predictions, one of which then happens immediately (see shading in Table 6):

	First prophecy	Second prophecy	Immediate fulfilment
'A man of God … of Judah' (13:1)	A descendant of David called Josiah will burn Jeroboam's fake priests on their fake altar (13:2).	'The altar shall be torn down, and the ashes . . . poured out' (13:3).	'The altar also was torn down, and the ashes poured out from the altar' (13:5).
'An old prophet lived in Bethel' (13:11)	The disobedient prophet from Judah will not be buried in his father's tomb (13:21–2).	Restatement of God's judgement against the altar at Bethel (13:32).	The disobedient prophet from Judah is killed by a lion on his way home (13:24).
Ahijah (14:2)	God will destroy the entire house of Jeroboam (14:10-11).	The moment Jeroboam's wife enters the city, his son will die (14:12).	When Jeroboam's wife arrives home, his son dies (14:17).

Table 6 **Two prophecies; one immediately fulfilled**

The effect of the immediate fulfilment of *one* of the prophecies each time is to strengthen our confidence that the other will also come to pass. The overall purpose of this section, then, is to show us that God responds to sin by speaking a word of judgement. And we can be sure that his prophetic word will be fulfilled. Judgement is inescapable.

In addition to this main point …

The first part of the story of 'the man of God [who] came out of Judah' (13:1–10) – let's call him Jude – emphasises the impotence of human efforts to thwart God's plans. As Jeroboam stretches out his hand to silence the prophet mid-prophecy ('Seize him,' verse 4) he is caught in a freeze frame, unable to move, until the very prophecy he wanted to stop has been accomplished. God's word will not be stopped. In the words of Captain Pete, the singing pirate in Phil Vischer's children's TV series, *What's in the Bible?*,[3]

> You can't stop a train by standing in the track
> You can't stop an avalanche by yelling, 'Hey, turn back!'
> And standing in the way of what God is gonna do
> Will be really, really, really, really not so good for you.

In the next scene, the modern reader easily fixates on Jude's plight (13:11–32). In line with God's instructions to him, he refuses a dinner invitation not once but twice (verses 8–10, 15–17), and gives in only because he accepts, in good faith, the word of another prophet (verse 18). It seems harsh that he should be mauled by a lion (verse 24), whereas the old prophet who lied to him so maliciously faces no sanction.

The AUTHOR'S PURPOSE TOOL must be our guide, however, for the text seems utterly uninterested in the ethics or motives of the deceitful old man. Instead, the emphasis is on the fact that Jude knew what God had said. This comes three times, the first two as the jam in a repeated sandwich (STRUCTURE TOOL meets REPETITION TOOL):[4]

> 'And I will not eat bread or drink water in this place,
>   *for so was it commanded me by the word of the Lord*, saying,
> "You shall neither eat bread nor drink water …"'

> 'I may not return with you … neither will I eat bread nor drink water with you in this place,
>   *for it was said to me by the word of the Lord*,
> "You shall neither eat bread nor drink water there, nor return by the way that you came."'
> (1 Kings 13:8–9, 16–17; see also 21–2)

---

[3] Thanks to Phil for giving us permission to quote from this excellent verse.

[4] Thanks to Richard Nelson, *First and Second Kings* (Louisville, KY: Westminster John Knox, 2012), p. 85, for pointing this out. Though we're less thankful for his assertion that the 'designation of Josiah by name is … obviously a prophecy made after the fact' (pp. 82–3). Sadly, this tells us far more about Mr Nelson's own presuppositions, viz. that God doesn't know the future, than about 1 Kings.

Ironically, it is Jude's death (which he himself caused!) that convinces the old man that Jude's message was true: a hungry lion sitting placidly beside an uneaten corpse bears the hallmarks of God's intervention.

Here's the point: if you know what God has said, then there is no excuse for believing something else. God's word will stand, whatever new 'revelations' may claim to supersede it.[5] God does not contradict himself.

So why are Christians still so gullible when it comes to novel theological ideas? Sometimes it is because of a misunderstanding of Jesus' words in John 16:13 ('When the Spirit of truth comes, he will guide you into all the truth'). This is read as if *the Church* is still being led into all truth; we haven't arrived there yet but are on an ongoing and evolving journey of 'doctrinal development'.[6] Thus a rogue contemporary voice tells us that 'the Apostle Paul might have said such and such in the first century, but the Holy Spirit has now led the Church to a fuller [i.e., totally different] understanding …' No! Any responsible reader of the 'WHO AM I?' TOOL will realise that Jesus was addressing his eleven apostles,[7] and promising that the Spirit would lead *them* into all truth. Far from encouraging doctrinal development, this verse teaches the Church to hold fast to the apostolic message as God's full and final revelation.

The final episode (14:1–20) focuses on Jeroboam's decision to consult the prophet Ahijah about the prognosis for his critically ill, and confusingly similarly named, son Abijah. This is the same Ahijah who had previously told Jeroboam that God hated Solomon's idolatry so much that he was giving Jeroboam most of the kingdom (CONTEXT TOOL, 1 Kings 11:29–39). Two golden calves later, Jeroboam has the chutzpah to ask a prophetic favour. Seemingly conscious that his sin may prevent a favourable hearing, we get five verses describing the elaborate disguise by which Jeroboam hopes his wife will trick the aged and blind Ahijah. His

---

[5] Even if they were to be spoken by 'an angel from heaven', Galatians 1:8.
[6] A phrase associated with the nineteenth-century Anglican convert to Roman Catholicism, John Henry Newman.
[7] Judas Iscariot having already left to betray him.

logic is horribly flawed: if it's that easy to pull the wool over Ahijah's eyes, then why go to the trouble of seeking his medical opinion in the first place? On the other hand, if he has divine insight ... In a delicious piece of comic timing, Ahijah calls out to her before she even rings the doorbell, 'Come in, wife of Jeroboam'!

Any note of comedy is quickly drowned out by the enormity of what Ahijah has to say. The child will die as a sign of the horrors that will befall the whole house of Jeroboam. If we think the child gets the raw deal here, we are mistaken. The wording of verse 13 in the ESV confused us at first: 'he only of Jeroboam shall come to the grave, because in him there is found something pleasing to the LORD'. Does this mean that everyone else in Jeroboam's family is immortal? And how is going to the grave a sign of God's favour? This is a good example of when to use the TRANSLATIONS TOOL, and the New Living Translation makes everything much clearer: 'He is the only member of your family *who will have a proper burial*' (emphasis added). This child gets off lightly. The others, by contrast, 'the dogs shall eat' or 'the birds of the heavens shall eat' (verse 11), a recurring theme in the book (see 16:4; 21:19, 23–4; 22:38; 2 Kings 9:10, 36).

Andrew recalls with delight a dramatisation of the scene by the students of Living Word Uganda, accompanied by a macabre rap:

> Hey Jeroboam, you think you're so wise
> Sending your wife to a prophet, in disguise,
> But God knows everything – he told me you had come
> And now, because you're evil, I have some-
> thing to say to you, yeah, now listen to my words,
> You're gonna be food for the dogs and the birds.[8]

Zooming out

Consider the connections to David's story. Ahijah was for Jeroboam both king maker and king breaker, just as Nathan had announced

---

8 Written by Andrew Sach. Used with permission.

to David both promises of blessing (2 Samuel 7) and judgement (2 Samuel 12). Jeroboam's son must die, just as did David's by Bathsheba. But note also the differences. David wept and prayed and repented. Jeroboam does none of these. Indeed, as David became the archetypal good king, so Jeroboam now becomes the archetypal villain.

Consider the connections to Jesus' story. We saw in Table 6 that when two things are predicted and one of them happens, you can be sure about the other. Jesus foretold both the destruction of the Temple and the end of the world in the same breath (e.g., Mark 13). The Temple was destroyed in AD 70. So it would be foolish to think he is bluffing about final judgement.

Good king, bad king
1 Kings 14:21 – 16:28

Back in the days when school involved a lot more learning by rote, British children used a rhyme to help them recall the kings and queens of England since 1066:

Willie, Willie, Harry, Stee,
Harry, Dick, John, Harry three;
One two three Neds, Richard two,
Harrys four five six ... then who?
[and a few kings later...]
Edward seven, George and Ted,
George the sixth, now Liz instead
(And now Charles III, though the rhyme didn't get that far)

Our creative skills have not extended to doing something similar with Rehoboam, Jeroboam, Abijam, Asa, Nadab, Baasha, Elah, Zimri, Omri and Tibni, but chapters 14–16 of the book of 1 Kings run through a succession of rulers of both Israel and Judah almost as fast as that old school mnemonic.

> **Dig deeper exercise**
> Use the AUTHOR'S PURPOSE TOOL.
> Why does the tempo of the narrative speed up so much in these two chapters, such that the author deals with the reigns of eight kings very quickly?
> Because similar phrases are used to describe each king, we cannot help but compare them: what repeated motifs can you identify?

Evil

All but one of the kings listed in these chapters is appraised negatively. Here is a catalogue of ungodly leadership. Using the REPETITION TOOL, we can pick out some of the recurring expressions:

'Did evil in the sight of the LORD'
'Walked in sin'
'Provoked the LORD to anger'

Next, there are the benchmarks. Abijam, king of Judah, is measured against the hero, David, but unfavourably. The kings of Israel are measured against 'Jeroboam, son of Nebat', who 'made Israel to sin'. They follow exactly in his footsteps.

Finally, there is the competitive aspect. Under the reign of Rehoboam, Judah manages to outdo 'all their fathers' in wickedness (14:22). But the prize goes to Omri who 'did more evil than all who were before him' (16:25).

Judgement

The author highlights the consequences of sin in various ways:

- Violent power struggles *within* Israel – there are three coups d'etat, with Baasha (15:27), Zimri (16:11) and Omri (16:17) all seizing the throne by force. Fun awaits the user of the TRANSLATIONS TOOL in 16:11 – have a look at the King James Version, which is the only English version that translates the Hebrew literally.[1] The Bible is often a lot less squeamish about the brutal realities of a sinful world than we are, but this colourful turn of phrase also tells us that amid the horror there is mercy for women and children.

---

1 The same expression occurs in 1 Samuel 25:22, 34; 1 Kings 14:10; 16:11; 21:21; 2 Kings 9:8. The sermon on YouTube on this topic by Steven Anderson had us in stitches, although (alarmingly) we're not sure he intended it to be funny. See 'Pastor Steven L Anderson Pisseth Against the Wall', YouTube: https://is.gd/pisseth (accessed 29 July 2024).

The divided kingdom

- Conflict *between* Israel and Judah (e.g., 14:30; 15:6, 7; 15:32) that at one stage gets so bad that Judah has to make an alliance with Syria over and against Israel!
- The de-glorification of the nation, as revealed by what happens to its gold. The CONTEXT TOOL reminds us of its history. Some dated back to the Exodus when they plundered their former slave masters (Exodus 12:35-6). More had arrived as tribute from the surrounding nations in the days of Solomon, prompting the Queen of Sheba's outburst of praise. Now some is grabbed by Shishak (14:25-6) and some given away to Ben Hadad in exchange for military help (15:18-19).
- The sign that God is behind this judgement, revealed twice by the intervention of his prophetic word (15:29 and 16:12).

Good

In contrast to assorted tyrants, Asa is a good king, with a heart like David. He got rid of some of the idols, and stopped his evil *grand-mother* (the most likely translation of 15:13 given 15:2). In some ways he foreshadows Josiah, the reformer, whom we will meet later.

Grace

There are two notes of God's grace in the passage. First, there is the reference to God placing his name at Jerusalem (14:21), reminding us of God's promise of forgiveness to those who pray to him at the Temple (CONTEXT TOOL, 8:27-53; 9:3). Second, there is the comfort that 'for David's sake' a lamp will remain burning in Jerusalem (15:4), a reminder of the promise of 2 Samuel 7.

Strikingly, neither of these positive notes is sounded during the reign of Asa, the good king, but rather during darker days. Whereas judgement follows sin, grace is wholly unrelated to any goodness in us.

The ups and (mainly) downs of history

There is nothing new under the sun. History continues to have its ups and downs, good rulers and (mainly) bad. In our lifetimes we have seen the likes of (listed in alphabetical order):

Angela Merkel, Barack Obama, Bashar al-Assad, Bill Clinton, Boris Johnson, Donald Trump, Ferdinand Marcos, George W. Bush, Hu Jintao, Idi Amin, Kim Jong Il, Muammar Gaddafi, Narendra Modi, Nelson Mandela, Nicolae Ceaușescu, Margaret Thatcher, Pol Pot, Queen Elizabeth II, Robert Mugabe, Slobodan Milošević, Tony Blair, Vladimir Putin, Xi Jinping. Among these are rulers who fear God, rulers who lead their nations into idolatry, rulers who humbly receive the crown, rulers who seize power, rulers who serve their people, rulers who exploit their people.

How Christians should rejoice in Christ Jesus, a King who resembles David and is nothing at all like Jeroboam. He is a King who never sinned or provoked the LORD to anger, a King who leads his people away from idolatry to worship the living and true God.

ELIJAH

Yahweh vs Baal: round 1
1 Kings 16:29 – 17:24

If they had published the *Guinness Book of World Records* in the ninth century BC, King Ahab would have got two entries:

> Ahab the son of Omri did evil in the sight of the LORD, more than all who were before him.
> (1 Kings 16:30)

> Ahab did more to provoke the LORD, the God of Israel, to anger than all the kings of Israel who were before him.
> (1 Kings 16:33)

Congratulations Ahab. You must be very proud. No one has ever been more evil, or made God more angry, than you!

What does he do that is so heinous?

> **Dig deeper exercise**
> Read 1 Kings 16:30–33
> Use the REPETITION TOOL? Which of Ahab's evil acts does the author emphasise?

Ahab worships a storm god ...

The false god Baal is mentioned more than forty times in the book of Kings. Archaeologists can also tell us lots about him thanks to excavations of a city called Ugarit in the 1930s. Among their discoveries is the rather handsome carving in Figure 7, now found in the Louvre in Paris. Baal was a storm god, to whom ancient peoples

Figure 7 **Baal with thunderbolt**
(Image: public domain)

would pray asking for rain and good harvest. As the museum's curator explained, 'The beautiful visual metaphor of the spear transformed into a plant is an allusion to the beneficial effects of the rain produced by storms.'[1]

Just think. What would be the most deliciously ironic way for Yahweh to expose Baal as a fake? Now read 1 Kings 17:1. Ha ha ha ha.

... so God announces a drought

It's all very well for Elijah to go to Ahab on a sunny day and announce that it's going to be a sunny day. Even the Met Office can reliably tell you what the weather is doing *now*. The prophecy

---

1 www.louvre.fr/en/oeuvre-notices/stela-depicting-storm-god-baal (accessed 1 August 2019).

becomes more impressive when, months later, there still isn't a cloud in the sky.

So why should Ahab take it seriously on day one?

Just beforehand comes a seemingly unrelated reference to a bloke called Hiel who tragically lost two sons while rebuilding the city of Jericho. Lest we miss the significance, the author tells us that this took place 'according to the word of the LORD, which he spoke by Joshua the son of Nun', the equivalent of him picking up the QUOTATION/ALLUSION TOOL and thrusting it into our hand (see Table 7)!

1 Kings 16:34	Joshua 6:26
'In his days Hiel of Bethel built Jericho.'	'Cursed before the LORD be the man who rises up and rebuilds this city, Jericho.'
'He laid its foundations at the cost of Abiram his firstborn,'	'At the cost of his firstborn shall he lay its foundation,'
'and set up its gates at the cost of his youngest, son, Segub.'	'and at the cost of his youngest son shall he set up its gates.'

Table 7 **A curse on the one who rebuilds Jericho**

By this time almost everyone would have forgotten the words of Joshua, but the author is reminding us that a promise God made hundreds of years earlier is fulfilled exactly. Why are we told this *here* (CONTEXT TOOL)? Surely to remind the reader that it's foolish to dismiss God's promises of judgement just because they lie in the future. If God declares a drought, Ahab shouldn't bet on a cold front coming off the Mediterranean any time soon.

As the months pass, we are told of riverbeds drying up (17:7), a famine so severe that a widow and her son face death by starvation (17:12), the pathetic sight of the king himself combing the length and breadth of the country to find so much as a tuft of grass to feed his horses (18:5).

Come on, Baal. This is your specialist area of expertise. We're not asking for a downpour, just a small shower. Even a light mist? The hygrometer is registering zero, Baal. Please help!

The score so far: Yahweh 1 – 0 Baal.

But God protects his prophet (and those who cling to his prophet)

If God's word is in control of the famine, it's also in control of famine relief for Elijah. What God says comes to pass.

- The word of the LORD came to Elijah, promising he would drink from the brook Cherith and be fed by the ravens (17:4). Sure enough, he drank from the brook Cherith and was fed by the ravens (17:6). More than two thousand years before Amazon thought of grocery deliveries by drone, God was sending care packages by bird.
- The word of the LORD came to Elijah promising that a widow would feed him (17:9). Sure enough, a widow, despite having almost no food of her own, agrees to feed him (17:11-15). It's just assumed by the Bible that God is as much in control of the lives of humans as the fate of birds (e.g., Matthew 6:26; 10:29).
- Elijah prophesied that the widow's 'jar of flour shall not be spent, and the jug of oil shall not be empty' (17:14). Sure enough 'the jar of flour was not spent, neither did the jug of oil become empty' (17:16). God very occasionally adjusts the laws of physics to help his people.

God's kindness to Elijah overflows to include the widow. For starters, as Elijah's caterer, she and her son get a share of the miraculously infinite supply of cake (17:15). But then tragedy strikes. Her son becomes ill and dies. As is common in bereavement, she experiences a mixture of anger and guilt (17:18). Is she getting what she deserves from Elijah's God? Elijah himself doesn't seem to think so (17:20), and when he calls out to God for mercy (17:21), Elijah receives power to raise the child from the dead (17:22-3).

This, of course, is amazing, but also very unusual – the first of only ten resurrections mentioned in the Bible (see if you can list the others without looking at the footnote[2]). The rarity of miracles

---

2 The others are a Shunamite's son (2 Kings 4:34); an unnamed Israelite whose funeral is

is key to understanding them correctly. They are not a blueprint for what the average Christian should expect. Few starving Christians receive famine-proof groceries, just as most grieving parents will not be reunited with their children in this life. It is a cruel pastor who suggests otherwise. They are unique signs in history that tell us something remarkable about the God who will one day make all things new. Even the widow of Zarephath, who *does* get her son back, learns a bigger lesson: 'the word of the LORD ... is truth' (17:24).

By now you will have come to appreciate that the author of Kings is a literary genius (it probably helped, to be fair, that he was divinely inspired) and never writes anything without a reason. So why the geography lesson in 17:9? If he had told us merely that she was 'from Zarephath', we'd think it was just setting the scene, but 'Zarephath, which belongs to Sidon' seems excessive. Why should we care about regional boundaries? Get out the CONTEXT TOOL and remind yourself of 16:31. Wow.

Here is a woman from the heartlands of Baal-worship. But Baal can't help her. It is the God of Elijah who comes to her aid, and by verse 24 she has become his disciple.

But there's a bittersweet irony here. A Baal-worshipper turns to Yahweh even as the people of Yahweh are turning to Baal. How often the genuine faith of the new convert shows up the fake religion of many in the pew! Indeed, Jesus used her example to illustrate this very point:

> And he said, 'Truly, I say to you, no prophet is acceptable in his home town. But in truth, I tell you, there were many widows in Israel in the days of Elijah, when the heavens were shut up three years and six months, and a great famine came

---

interrupted by a Moabite invasion (2 Kings 13:21); the widow of Nain's son (Luke 7:15); Jairus' daughter (Luke 8:55); Lazarus (John 11:44); a whole cemetery full of people at the time of Jesus' death (Matthew 27:52); Jesus himself (see all of the Gospels); Tabitha (Acts 9:40); Eutychus, who fell out of an upstairs window to his death during a long sermon (Acts 20:10–12). A friend of ours also suggested that Moses and Elijah must have been resurrected for them to show up on the Mount of Transfiguration (Matthew 17:3). If so, that would make it twelve.

over all the land, and Elijah was sent to none of them but only to Zarephath, in the land of Sidon, to a woman who was a widow.'
(Luke 4:24–6)

Yahweh vs Baal: round 2
1 Kings 18

After Baal's humiliation in the Rain Competition, Elijah now challenges the 450 prophets of Baal to round 2: a Barbeque Competition. The rules are simple. Each side gets to prepare its own firewood, then cuts a cow into steaks and lays them out on the grill. But no one is allowed firelighters. Or matches for that matter. Or flints. They just have to pray to their respective God/god and ask him to send fire from heaven. Heavenly ignition, if you will (verses 23–6).

Baal's prophets pray all morning (verse 26), but since Baal proved incapable of sending so much as a drop of water during the three-year drought, it's no surprise that he can't manage a spark before lunch. So Elijah starts to have some fun with them: 'Shout a bit louder! Maybe Baal is a bit deaf? Or maybe he's deep in thought? Or on the loo? Or he's gone travelling? Or he's dozed off and you need to wake him up?' (verse 27).

None of these excuses is very appropriate for someone you'd want to worship, and so when Elijah says, 'for he is a god' (verse 27), we discern a wry sarcasm. Desperate to salvage their spiritual credibility, the prophets then resort to self-harm, slashing themselves in the hope that blood sacrifice might coerce the dozy deity into action. It doesn't. To quote verse 29 verbatim, 'There was no voice. No one answered; no one paid attention.'

So now it's Elijah's turn. Before praying to Yahweh, he first orders that his altar be doused liberally with water. Why? Perhaps because after three years with no rain, the wood is so dry that even a boy scout would find it insulting to be challenged to light it, let alone the true and living God. At least this way it requires a miracle

Elijah

worthy of his time. And given the scarcity of drinking water, expending so much on the contest certainly raises the stakes for the Israelites. If Yahweh doesn't come through for them soon, they are in all kinds of trouble.

Then a short prayer and PSSHWZZ! The wood is ablaze, the water evaporates, the stones are vaporised (apparently this requires a temperature of around 3,000 degrees Celsius), and the roast beef is turned into smoke that rises to delight God's nostrils. And everyone falls on their faces in worship.

It's Yahweh 2 – 0 Baal.

And then it rains.

Here's a question though: why does God wait until he has decisively won the Barbecue Competition before he scores the winning goal in the Rain Competition? Anyone equipped with the STRUCTURE TOOL will already be wondering that:

verses 1–19	Elijah meets Ahab; no rain.
verses 20–40	Showdown with the prophets of Baal.
verses 41–6	Elijah meets Ahab again; rain.

There's an obvious answer. If the rain had come any earlier, Baal's supporters could have taken credit: 'Praise be to the storm god who finally sent the storm!' It's only safe to fill the sky with clouds *after* Baal has been trounced and everyone confessed that Yahweh is the true God.

All very good. Except that we haven't taken the AUTHOR'S PURPOSE TOOL very seriously at all. We've described the main events of the chapter, and given our own explanation of them, but in doing so we've completely missed the point he is making.

The fact is, the competition isn't between Yahweh and Baal at all, for the simple reason that *Baal doesn't exist*.[1] Imagine I told you that I recently won a game of tennis.

'Oh?' you reply. 'Who were you playing against?'

---

[1] Just as the New Testament assures us 'an idol has no real existence' (1 Corinthians 8:4). That's not to deny that demons are real, and the worship of false gods is a demonic thing (1 Corinthians 10:19–22).

1 Kings 18

'No one. I won in straight sets. He didn't even return my serve.'
'So what you're saying is you beat no one at all?'
To defeat Baal is a nonsense. Something else has been going on.
Let's begin by using the STRUCTURE TOOL more carefully. There's more to say about the 'before' and 'after' than simply the story of a drought (verses 1, 5) followed by a storm (verses 41–6)(see Table 8).

Before Yahweh sends fire	After Yahweh sends fire
When polled with the simplest of all theological questions – 'Who is God: Yahweh or Baal?' – the people are stumped (verse 21). They are enthusiastic about the Barbecue Competition (verse 24), presumably because they hope it might help them decide between deities.	The people are in no doubt who the real God is, falling on their faces to declare, 'The LORD, he is God; the LORD, he is God' (verse 39).

Table 8 What changes at Mount Carmel?

The change doesn't concern Baal himself, who doesn't appear in the script. It's a change in the *people*.

Once we realise that, a whole lot of other details fall into place. Take the fact that Elijah repairs an altar to the LORD using twelve stones ...

Dig deeper exercise

Read 1 Kings 18:30–32 and use the NARRATOR'S COMMENT TOOL. Why is the number twelve important here?

We need to be careful not to over-interpret every number in the Bible. If you don't believe us, try googling '666'. Actually, please don't. However, encouraged by the interpretative steer you picked up from your Dig Deeper exercise, we are emboldened to see something symbolic also in the four jars poured three times (do the maths! $4 \times 3 = 12$). Everything is meant to remind them who they are as the twelve tribes of Israel, the people of Yahweh. If it were an episode of *Sesame Street*, we might say that it had been brought by the letter Y and the number twelve.

The symbolic numbers are quickly followed by what we call a 'horizontal prayer'. You know, the kind that is half directed towards God and half towards the others in the prayer meeting. 'Thank you, Lord, that you have blessed our church with ample parking for the morning service, *provided that everyone stays within the lines!*'

> O LORD, God of Abraham, Isaac, and Israel, let it be known this day that you are God in Israel, and that I am your servant, and that I have done all these things at your word. Answer me, O LORD, answer me, that this people may know that you, O LORD, are God, and that you have turned their hearts back. (1 Kings 18:36–7)

We might be a little squeamish about the slaughter of the 450 prophets of Baal that follows the divine barbecue in verse 40, but in fact Elijah is acting rightly. Deuteronomy 13 mandated the death penalty for false prophets who led the people into idolatry, and a careful comparison of verse 21 and 26 reveals just how much Baal worship had corrupted Israel. The people are 'limping' between two opinions, just as the false prophets 'limped' around their altar.[2] When Elijah asked the people to choose the true deity, they 'did not answer', just as 'no one answered' the false prophets' prayers. This just execution of false prophets is a marked contrast to the cruel martyrdom of true prophets by Jezebel back in verse 4.

We are now ready for the big reveal. We asked earlier why God waited until after the Barbecue Competition to send the rain. And there's a much more profound answer. We'd love you to enjoy the 'Aha' moment for yourself so we simply suggest that you use the CONTEXT TOOL and reread 1 Kings 8:35–6.

This chapter is a wake-up call. We may not be tempted to worship Baal, but 'limping between two different opinions' is still a danger. Serving Jesus on Sunday, serving money on Monday. Loving Jesus, loving my non-Christian girlfriend. It's what James refers to as

---

[2] You may not see the parallel if you're using a less literal translation, but it's there in the original Hebrew.

'double-mindedness' (James 1:8; 4:8), and he warns that 'whoever wishes to be a friend of the world makes himself an enemy of God' (James 4:4). It's no less serious for the New Testament Church than for Old Testament Israel, and 1 Kings 18 is a good antidote. God is the living and true God. He punishes those who turn to idols and blesses those who repent.

There's more than one way to be a hero

As we picked up the COPYCAT TOOL, we realised that while Elijah is clearly a hero of this chapter, he's not the *only* hero. Those of us who find his boldness intimidating, who feel inadequate that our own service of the Lord is quieter and more behind-the-scenes, will surely be encouraged by the example of Obadiah. He's not as brave as Elijah. Indeed, he is horrified at his friend's suggestion that they go together to confront Ahab, fretting that he will 'kill me' (three times! verses 9, 12, 14) and asking, 'What have I done to deserve this?' I (Andrew) think of how I winced as my evangelist friend, Ziggy 'Elijah' Rogoff, sat diagonally across from me on the London Underground on the way home from a talk I had given, and began a loud conversation – 'THANKS FOR EXPLAINING HOW JESUS ROSE FROM THE DEAD, ANDREW' – with the express intention of being overheard by our fellow passengers.

Yet, though Obadiah is scared of Ahab, he fears the LORD *more* – and for that the author gives him a big thumbs up (verse 3). Fear of the LORD makes even timid Christians do very courageous things. Thus Obadiah hides a hundred prophets in two caves to keep them safe from Jezebel's lynch mob, smuggling them food and water (verse 4) – a kind of ninth-century BC version of Corrie ten Boom. Then, despite his misgivings, he agrees to puts his life on the line and brokers a meeting between Ahab and the firebrand Elijah.

Hooray for the Elijahs of the world. But also hooray for the Obadiahs. Role models, the pair of them.

Elijah was a man just like us?

Having said this, there's a very particular way in which all of us can be Elijahs.

Hands up if your prayers have ever changed the weather system of an entire region for three years? Or gained you an audience with the Prime Minister? Thought not. No one equipped with the 'WHO AM I?' TOOL would suggest that Elijah gives us a normative example of the power of prayer. Would they?

> The prayer of a righteous person has great power as it is working. Elijah was a man with a nature like ours, and he prayed fervently that it might not rain, and for three years and six months it did not rain on the earth. Then he prayed again, and heaven gave rain, and the earth bore its fruit.
> (James 5:16b–18)

What is going on? James is an apostle, so he must be right, but does that mean that we've got the Bible toolkit completely wrong? Keep reading; in the very next verses (CONTEXT TOOL) James goes on to explain in what sense our prayers might be like Elijah's:

> My brothers [and sisters], if anyone among you wanders from the truth and someone brings him back, let him know that whoever brings back a sinner from his wandering will save his soul from death and will cover a multitude of sins.
> (James 5:19–20)

We may not ever see God's fire falling from the sky, but, just like Elijah, we can pray for those around us to turn back to the Lord. God is gracious. These are the kinds of prayers he loves to answer.

Maybe you can think of a friend who once burned white-hot with zeal for Jesus. But you haven't seen them at church for a while. Actually, now you come to think of it, you've not seen them at church for months and months. You're worried that they are drifting. Why not take a moment to do an Elijah and pray that the Lord would turn their heart back?

The still, small voice
1 Kings 19

Even spiritual giants can experience burnout. Elijah has just witnessed the most amazing revival atop Mount Carmel. But all he feels is despair. 'O LORD, take away my life,' he prays. 'I've failed.'

Come on Elijah, you've just defeated 450 prophets of Baal! Fire fell from heaven: it was awesome! Don't you remember the people shouting, 'The LORD, he is God; the LORD, he is God'? Why are you so down?

The best treatment for depression isn't always pharmaceutical or cognitive-behavioural (although it may include both of these). Sometimes what you need more than anything is rest. Thus, Elijah collapses exhausted under a broom tree and sleeps. With great tenderness, God dispatches an angel with his breakfast – a 'cake baked on hot stones' (verse 6), which sounds like something you could find only in Waitrose.[1] He sleeps again. Then God sends him on a pilgrimage to a quiet cave in the mountains where, instead of theological pyrotechnics (the last thing that he needs), the LORD speaks to him in a 'still small voice' (KJV). To quote the Christian hymn:

> Breathe through the heats of our desire
> Thy coolness and Thy balm;
> Let sense be dumb, let flesh retire;
> Speak through the earthquake, wind, and fire,
> O still, small voice of calm.[2]

---

[1] For international readers, Waitrose is one of the more expensive supermarkets in the UK, known for its gourmet fayre.
[2] John Greenleaf Whittier (1807–92), 'Dear Lord and Father of Mankind'.

No wonder this chapter has been a favourite of Christian counsellors. Yet this way of reading it is almost entirely wrong.

Please don't misunderstand us. We aren't denying that godly Christians can struggle with depression. They can. Nor do we doubt that God deals gently with the downhearted, as Isaiah says so beautifully of Jesus: 'a bruised reed he will not break, and a faintly burning wick he will not quench' (Isaiah 42:3). It's simply – as the AUTHOR'S PURPOSE TOOL helps us to see – that that is not the point *here*.

If God were simply trying to restore Elijah's soul, why send him on the ninth-century BC version of the Marathon des Sables? He's safe from Queen Jezebel as soon as he crosses the border into Judah (verse 3), and there are closer holiday destinations than Mount Horeb, a forty-day trek across the desert (verse 8). Indeed, the angel's stated reason for providing the stone-baked loaf is the arduousness of this journey (verse 7). Then when he finally arrives at the famous mountain, God tells him to recruit some assassins. It's difficult to believe this is intended primarily as a form of restorative therapy.

Let's try to dig a little deeper.

Silence that speaks volumes

Elijah's strange encounter with God at Mount Horeb is the heart of the passage. It begins with a brief interview, during which Elijah describes the spiritual state of the nation. Sometimes people say he's lost perspective – he's feeling down and that colours everything. Let's evaluate his evaluation.

'I have been very jealous for the LORD, the God of hosts.' This is one for the VOCABULARY TOOL. Jealousy can be bad when it refers to wanting what belongs to someone else (e.g., Genesis 37:11; Psalm 106:16). More often in the Bible the word refers to God wanting what is rightfully his – he refuses to share his glory with idols or false gods (e.g., Deuteronomy 4:23–4; 5:8–9; 6:14–15). Elijah is right to be jealous on God's behalf, just as the Apostle Paul was rightly 'provoked' by the pagan shrines of Athens (Acts 17:16).

'The people of Israel have forsaken your covenant, thrown down your altars, and killed your prophets with the sword.' We read evidence of all three crimes in the previous chapter. But wasn't that before they repented? Why so gloomy *now*? In fact, Elijah is right to be pessimistic. The spiritual fate of the nation rests with the king, and for as long as wicked Ahab remains on the throne and his idolatrous wife Jezebel continues her campaign of persecution against the faithful, there can be no lasting spiritual change. Indeed, by the time we reach 2 Kings 10, the cancer of Baal worship has again spread everywhere.

'I, even I only, am left.' Come now, Elijah, surely you're exaggerating? What about Obadiah and the hundred that he hid in caves? Or the 6,998 others that we find out about in verse 18?

Yet even here, Elijah is right in one sense. His maths isn't as flawed as we might think. For when he stood up to Ahab he said, 'I, even I only, am left a prophet of the LORD, but Baal's prophets are 450 men' (CONTEXT TOOL, 18:22). And he really was the only one taking a *public* stand, a lone voice of orthodoxy challenging the national consensus. Like when Martin Luther opposed the Holy Roman Empire at the Diet of Worms, or Dietrich Bonhoeffer defied the Nazis. He must have felt very alone.

And then finally, 'they seek my life, to take it away.' No arguing with that (see verse 2)!

God's question and Elijah's response come twice, which gets us reaching for the STRUCTURE TOOL:

Q. What are you doing here, Elijah? (verse 9)
A. Israel has broken the covenant (verse 10)

> God's response part 1: earthquake/wind/fire/quiet voice (verses 11–12)

Q. What are you doing here, Elijah? (verse 13)
A. Israel has broken the covenant (verse 14)

> God's response part 2: send the assassins (verses 15–18)

Elijah

It reminds us of one of those choose-your-own-adventure stories that were popular when we were teenagers in the 1990s (oops, gave away our ages there). At the end of every page, you get to decide what happens next from a couple of options: 'To hide in a cave and watch a whirlwind go by, turn to page 473,' or, 'To recruit three hitmen, turn to page 381.' Often, though, you eventually end up back in the same place regardless of what you pick. That's the case here. All roads lead to assassins. Nothing that happens on top of the mountain can avert that.

So what is the point of the fireworks on Mount Horeb?

Verses 11–12 are well known but not well understood. We must let the author direct our interpretation, and not take shortcuts to something we *expect* him to say. The two most obvious features in the text seem to be:

1. Clear allusions to Exodus (QUOTATION/ALLUSION TOOL) (see Table 9):
2. A clear *contrast* to Exodus, readily detected using the REPETITION TOOL: 'the LORD was *not* in the wind … *not* in the earthquake … *not* in the fire' (verses 11–12).

1 Kings 19	Corresponding feature in Exodus	Significance in Exodus
God sends Elijah to Mount Horeb (verse 8) where there is wind, earthquake and fire (verses 11–12).	The people of Israel go to Mount Sinai (another name for Mount Horeb*), where there is an earthquake and fire (Exodus 19:16–20).	God made his covenant with the people of Israel (Exodus 19:5–6).
Elijah hides in a cave (verse 9) as God 'passed by' (verse 11).	Moses hid in a cleft of the rock as God 'passed by' (Exodus 33:22).	God renewed the covenant after the people of Israel broke it by worshipping a golden calf (Exodus 34:10, 27).

Table 9 **Back to Sinai**

* In Exodus 3:1 it's called Horeb, and in verse 12 Moses is told that he will return to 'this' mountain. When they do return it's called Sinai (19:11).

1 Kings 19

Putting these together, it seems the LORD has brought Elijah to the covenant mountain; not just where the covenant was made but also where it was *re*made after an earlier crisis in Israel's history. No wonder Elijah was willing to make the 260-mile journey. This could be just the second chance they need. All we need is for God to pass by, do the earthquake and fire thing, and the relationship will be back on track. Except … it doesn't happen. God isn't in it.

A common interpretation of verse 12b is that, after not being in the wind, earthquake and fire, God *is* in the 'low whisper'.

There are several problems with this view. First, the text simply doesn't say this. Second, a sentimental preference for quiet voices is hard to square with the many places in the Bible where God says important things very loudly (e.g., Deuteronomy 5:22; Luke 23:46 or virtually anything said by an angel in the book of Revelation). Third, God showing up in an earthquake and fire was very good news back in Exodus 19. Tranquillity doesn't improve on this epic drama. It's a terrifying anticlimax because of the renewed promises that God *doesn't* make.

Surely something is said, though? After all, 'Elijah heard it' (verse 13). Our guess is that the barely audible sound is a muffled version (around fifty decibels quieter because of the cavernous acoustic) of the words Elijah will hear more clearly when he emerges from the depths of the cave: 'What are you doing here, Elijah?'

In case you're confused, here's a paraphrase of the whole thing:

> Elijah came to a cave on Mount Sinai, where Moses had received the covenant, and where the covenant had been renewed after Israel's apostasy with a golden calf. And God said to him, 'What are you doing here, Elijah?' He replied, 'Your people have broken your covenant.' And God told him that he would 'pass by', just as he had done with Moses. And behold an earthquake, just as there had been at the time of Moses – but wait, something's wrong; God isn't in the earthquake. Then fire, just as there had been at the time of Moses – but wait, something's wrong; God isn't in the fire. And Elijah wondered whether God might renew the covenant and

provide new stone tablets and give them a second chance, just as he had done with Moses. But no. Instead, he heard just an indistinct whisper, which, when he came to the entrance of the cave to hear more clearly, turned out to be God repeating the same question, 'What are you doing here, Elijah?' He replied, 'Your people have broken your covenant.'

This time God announces a verdict. His response to Israel's apostasy is to bring terrible judgement through Hazael, Jehu and Elisha (verses 15–17), a triumvirate of divinely appointed assassins. We see this judgement played out in the first ten chapters of 2 Kings, and it is bloody and horrific. Nevertheless, in wrath God remembers mercy, and he will spare a faithful remnant (verse 18; see also Romans 11:4–5).

No sooner have God's executioners been named than we meet one of them. In a dramatic final scene, Elijah casts his mantle on Elisha son of Shaphat, who at once abandons his farm, turning his entire herd into a burnt offering (verse 21), and follows him.

Enough is enough

Back in Exodus, when it was Moses rather than Elijah occupying the famous cave, God had proclaimed his name:

> The LORD, the LORD, a God merciful and gracious, slow to anger, and abounding in steadfast love and faithfulness, keeping steadfast love for thousands, forgiving iniquity and transgression and sin, but who will by no means clear the guilty, visiting the iniquity of the fathers on the children and the children's children, to the third and the fourth generation.
> (Exodus 34:6–7)

It's arguably the most important paragraph in the Old Testament. At least, the rest of the Old Testament seems to think so – it's quoted often (e.g., Nehemiah 9:17; Psalm 86:15; 103:8; 145:8; Joel

2:13; Jonah 4:2). It tells us that God is *slow* to anger. He doesn't have a short fuse.

Yet even a long fuse burns down eventually. So when 'Ahab did more to provoke the LORD, the God of Israel, to anger than all the kings of Israel who were before him' (1 Kings 16:33), God's patience eventually ran out. Enough is enough. Second chances, yes. Infinite chances, no.

Dig deeper exercise

This is going to be an exercise in how *not* to use the BIBLE TIMELINE TOOL. Usually, it's helpful to ask what has changed as we move from the Old Testament to the New Testament. But sometimes nothing has changed.

How might a wrong understanding of Jesus' forgiveness be used to cancel out the warnings of 1 Kings?

Look up Romans 11:17-22; 1 Corinthians 10:1-13; Hebrews 2:1-4. How would you apply warnings not to fall away to someone at our point in the timeline?

The owardice of King Ahab
1 Kings 20 – 21

Bully-boy Ben-hadad and a big God (1 Kings 20:1–43)

In the summer of 2021, as a resurgent Taliban started taking over part of Afghanistan, President Ashraf Ghani vowed to 'fight to the death'. By 15 August, as the Taliban neared Kabul, Ghani fled, reportedly taking bags full of money with him.

On 24 February 2022, Russia invaded Ukraine. The next day, as bombs rained down on Kyiv and the satellite imagery revealed a forty-mile(!) line of Russian tanks, the United States offered to airlift President Volodymyr Zelensky and his family to safety. But he refused to leave, telling the West, 'The fight is here. I need ammunition, not a ride.'[1]

Whatever flaws Zelensky may have, he will be remembered for his bravery. And whatever virtues Ghani may have, he will be remembered for his spinelessness.

King Ahab is more of a Ghani. When Ben-hadad, king of Syria threatens him, demanding tribute, he grovels and gives in: 'As you say, my lord, O king, I am yours, and all I have' (20:4).

If you don't stand up to bullies, they just get worse. Therefore Ben-hadad, smelling weakness, pushes further and asks for more (verses 5–6). Ahab freaks out and gathers all the elders of Israel for moral support in verse 7. They persuade him to refuse the enemy's demands, leading to some sabre rattling and trash talking (verse

---

1 Sharon Braithwaite, 'Zelensky refuses US offer to evacuate, saying "I need ammunition, not a ride"', CNN, 26 February 2022: edition.cnn.com/2022/02/26/europe/ukraine-zelensky-evacuation-intl (accessed 30 July 2024).

10), of the kind that boxers throw at one another before a bout. Alasdair's favourite example of the genre is a well-known quip from the great Muhammed Ali that you'll find in this footnote.[2] Ahab's version is notably less self-assured: 'Let not him who straps on his armour boast himself as he who takes it off' (verse 11). We might paraphrase, 'Don't get ahead of yourself', or, 'It isn't over until it's over.'

But the reader supposes that it will very soon be over. Ahab is an evil king, and we are awaiting disaster at the hands of Elisha, Hazael or Jehu, the hitmen named in the previous episode. Or maybe it will be Ben-hadad who deals the killer blow?

Instead, in a major plot twist, a prophet appears out of nowhere and promises that God will give Syria into Ahab's hand (verse 13). Bizarrely, he stipulates that rather than sending in the Marines or the Paras or the SAS, Ahab must draft his army, or at least the vanguard, from the servants of the regional governors (there are only 232 of them). There's no way a team of gardeners and valets, heralds and pages, marshals and butlers is going to win unless by divine intervention. And that's the point. God does it so that Ahab will *'know that I am the Lord'* (verse 13, emphasis added).

After a surprising triumph, the prophet urges Ahab not to rest on his laurels but to prepare for a renewed Syrian offensive in the spring (verse 22).

Meanwhile the enemy's strategists do some hard thinking and determine that the reason they lost the previous battle was that the Israelite 'gods' are 'gods of the hills' (verse 23). If they take the fight to the plains, then these 'gods' will be powerless, right? Oh dear. The Syrians do seem to have rather underestimated the God who made the world and everything in it.

Again the odds seem heavily against the Israelites. When the author portrays them as 'goats' (verse 27) before a vast army, they sound as if they are destined for the slaughter. There's no way

---

[2] 'Frazier's got two chances. Slim, and none. And Slim just left town.' Cited in 'The Greatest Boxing Trash Talk Of All Time', Shortlist, https://www.shortlist.com/news/the-greatest-boxing-trash-talk-of-all-time (accessed 12 August 2024).

they're going to win unless by divine intervention. And that's the point. God does it to show the Syrians that the 'god of the hills' is not too shabby at fighting in the valleys! And so that Ahab will '*know that I am the Lord*' (verse 28, emphasis added).

Having spotted that same phrase yet again, we sense that the author is making a deliberate point, and the QUOTATION/ALLUSION TOOL reveals what it is: these words are lifted straight from the book of Exodus (see Exodus 6:7; 7:5, 17; 8:22; 10:2; 14:4, 18; 16:12; 29:46). God delivered the Israelites from slavery in Egypt, and provided for them in the wilderness, and dwelt in their midst 'so that you will know that I am the LORD'.

What a surprising phrase to find *here*! Elijah's abortive trip to Sinai suggested that God had had enough; his fuse had burned down all the way. And yet he shows *still more* kindness to the apostate king! The enemy sustains huge losses (verses 29–30), with the fatal toppling of the wall being an unmistakable sign of God's involvement (Joshua 6 vibes?).

All Ahab has to do now is to finish Ben-hadad off. But he's too weak to do so. The story of how an unnamed prophet exposes the king's failure (verses 35–42) is quite involved, but brilliant, and we urge you to read it for yourself. Note in passing another lion mauling (the same thing happened in 13:24–8 when God's word was ignored). Note the signature 'Nathan' move (see 2 Samuel 12:1–7) whereby the prophet sneakily gets Ahab to pass judgement on (he thinks) a soldier who has failed in his duty, and thereby unwittingly to pass judgement on himself. Note also the summary in verse 42: Ahab's life is now forfeit.

The king's response? To go off in an enormous sulk (verse 43).

Jezebel and a poor Jezreelite (1 Kings 21:1–24)

The next instalment of the drama is linked to the previous one by Ahab's foul mood. This time he is 'vexed and sullen' (the wording is the same in 20:43 and 21:4) as a result of Naboth's refusal to sell him the family vineyard. The law of Moses forbade any permanent sale of an Israelite's land, as Ahab should have known.³

Jezebel is keen to lift her husband's spirits, so she devises a plan to remove Naboth from the equation. It's a grim irony that the queen, who doesn't give a single thought to the LORD or his law, uses false witnesses to testify that Naboth has broken the law, in order to get him killed (the penalty for blasphemy was death by stoning). Under the guise of punishing evil she perpetrates a terrible evil. In the name of righteousness, unrighteousness.⁴

Ahab doesn't rebuke his wife or mourn the death of Naboth. He simply goes to take the vineyard. He's got what he wanted and there's no point losing sleep over the grubby methods. Jezebel has worked hard to give him plausible deniability for the murder, but it really isn't very plausible, and he doesn't even try to deny it.

So God sends Ahab's nemesis, Elijah:

> Arise, go down to meet Ahab king of Israel, who is in Samaria; behold, he is in the vineyard of Naboth, where he has gone to take possession. And you shall say to him, 'Thus says the LORD, "Have you killed and also taken possession?"'
> (1 Kings 21:18-19)

It's striking that when God wanted to intervene in a war, an unnamed prophet would do, but in response to the death of an apparently unimportant vineyard-owner from Jezreel, God sends in the A-lister. God is bothered about the little people.

---

3 See Leviticus 25:14-34.

4 The central principle in Israel's courts was 'eye for eye, tooth for tooth', such that punishment should be meted out in proportion to the crime. You don't receive the death penalty for stealing a loaf of bread. But you do for murder and for blasphemy, since God is worthy of more honour even than a human life. See Leviticus 24:13-23. But perhaps anticipating how the law might be weaponised by the likes of Jezebel, Moses specified that in cases of a false witness, 'you shall do to him as he had meant to do to his brother' again on the 'eye for eye, tooth for tooth' principle (Deuteronomy 19:18-21).

Sins of omission

Something has been missing in our talk of Naboth and Ben-hadad thus far. Namely the letter 'c'. Thanks to an absurd dare by an Aussie friend, we managed to write the whole thing up until now without using the third letter of the alphabet.[5]

But there's also a point to it. In these chapters, Ahab is not guilty primarily of sins of *commission* but of sins of *omission*. The problem is what's missing, what he fails to do. As the 1662 Book of Common Prayer puts it:

> We have left undone those things,
> which we ought to have done;
> and we have done those things
> which we ought not to have done;
> and there is no health in us.[6]

Ahab fails to do anything about Ben-hadad in chapter 20 and fails to do anything about Jezebel in chapter 21. It's striking that she is the one who commits the murder, and yet the Lord lays the charge at *his* door (21:19; compare Eve eating the fruit and Adam receiving from God the consequent death penalty in Genesis 3 and Romans 5:12). Failure to take responsibility for his wife's actions is a serious evil.

He is a weak man. He wants an easy life and refuses to take responsibility. God judges him for his sinful passivity and describes in stark terms: 'you have sold yourself to do what is evil in the sight of the Lord' (21:20).

Let's take up the 'so what?!' tool and consider how to apply all of this to ourselves.

---

5 'You have to include an Easter Egg in the book,' urged Nick Duke. 'You can get ChatGPT to help.' Andrew thought this was a great idea and instructed the AI engine to 'rewrite the following chapter, without including any words that contain the letter "c"'. Unfortunately, GPT-4.0 wasn't intelligent enough to do this and failed spectacularly. But by this time Andrew was in far too deep, and stayed up half the night with a thesaurus …

6 'Morning Prayer from The Book of Common Prayer'; justus.anglican.org/~ss/commonworship/word/morningbcp.html (accessed 30 July 2024).

On the one hand, we can thank God that we are ruled by the Lord Jesus, and not by Ahab. Jesus never shirked responsibility. He will not fail to destroy the Ben-hadads that threaten his people. Nor will he turn a blind eye when Naboths in the church are oppressed.

As a secondary application, though, we must repent of our own passivity and sometimes *cowardice*. This is one of the sins listed in Revelation 21:8 as a reason for people being excluded from the heavenly Jerusalem. It's serious for men to fail to take a lead in their families. It's serious to fail to stand up for what we know is right, for an easy life. It's serious to fail to follow through on God's commands. Sometimes we think of courage only in terms of willingness to put oneself in physical danger (on a battlefield, for example). But we must not neglect the importance of moral courage.

> **Dig deeper exercise**
>
> Read God's sentence of punishment against Ahab in 21:17–24. Use the CONTEXT TOOL. How does this paragraph bring to a climax some canine and avian horrors we have seen before in 1 Kings (see 14:11 and 16:4)?
> What do we expect to happen next?
> What, rather surprisingly, does in fact happen next (21:25–9)?

Shocking grace (1 Kings 21:25–9)

Astonishingly, the most evil king in Israel's history repents. More surprising still is God's evident delight in it. He tells Elijah in the same way your aunt Susan told all her neighbours when you passed your grade 3 trumpet exam: Elijah, have you seen this? Look at this! (verse 29). His response is to defer disaster to the next generation (just as he did for Solomon in 11:12).

It is too much to see this as a full-blown anticipation of the gospel. God is only delaying the dog-licking-up-blood end to Ahab that he will still bring in chapter 22. But it is grace nonetheless. The point is clear: God loves it when someone humbles himself before him, however appalling their deeds have been until that point.

The prophet who refused to scratch where they itched

1 Kings 22:1–50

As we write this chapter, it's the beginning of hay fever season. We've got itchy eyes and itchy noses. Alasdair is grateful that he is working with Andrew via video link because Andrew has just sneezed fulsomely directly into the camera (where Alasdair's face would have been in real life). In biblical terms, however, itchy *ears* are far more serious: 'The time is coming when people will not endure sound teaching, but having itching ears they will accumulate for themselves teachers to suit their own passions' (2 Timothy 4:3).

In this chapter of 1 Kings, Ahab faces a choice between what he knows to be true and what he would *like* to be true (but knows to be false). You can almost feel his ears itch as you follow the drama, scene by scene.

God's word through the prophet Micaiah goes head to head with what we might call an 'anti-word' from the four hundred other prophets. The STRUCTURE TOOL helps us to see this, because part of the text runs in parallel (see Table 10).

Suspense mounts. Having weighed the advice, will he in fact go to battle against Ramoth-gilead, or will he refrain? But we don't want to get ahead of ourselves. Let's begin at scene one.

Ahab's failure, back in chapter 20, to follow through with the God-given victory over the Syrians now comes back to haunt him, and three years later he decides to try to finish the job. This time he enlists the help of Jehoshaphat, king of Judah. We are reminded that Judah and its kings are not as far gone as Israel, as

1 Kings 22:1–50

'Shall I go to battle against Ramoth-gilead, or shall I refrain?' (verse 6).	'Micaiah, shall we go to Ramoth-gilead to battle, or shall we refrain?' (verse 15).
The anti-word: you will win.	The true word: you will lose.
The human court in session before the kings of Israel and Judah (verse 10).	The heavenly court in session before the LORD (verse 19).
Zedekiah offers his own prophecy (verse 11).	Zedekiah opposes Micaiah's prophecy (verse 24).

Table 10 **Shall I go to battle or not?**

Jehoshaphat wisely suggests that before going to war, they 'enquire first for the word of the LORD'. This had apparently not occurred to Ahab.

Ahab duly fetches four hundred prophets, who all tell him what he wants to hear. This immediately strikes us as suspicious, since the LORD has previously found one prophet at a time to be quite sufficient – Moses, Samuel, Nathan, Elijah, etc. Jehoshaphat is suspicious too and asks rather pointedly whether there is 'another prophet *of the Lord*' (verse 7, emphasis added), implying that Ahab's seers may have other allegiances.[1] Ahab grudgingly acknowledges that there is another, but complains that he 'never prophesies good concerning me, but evil' (verse 8). Evidently the criterion by which Ahab selects counsellors is how adept they are at flattery; truth-telling is secondary.

Jehoshaphat holds his ground, and Micaiah is summoned. Meanwhile, we are treated to the equivalent of a full Broadway stage show by the four hundred. The Tony Award goes to Zedekiah, who adorns himself with home-made iron horns to supplement his false words with a visual display of the supposed victory to come (verse 11). Perhaps this will help to persuade Ahab to believe what he wants to believe.

Scene two, when Micaiah arrives, is structured around the three words that Micaiah speaks:

---

[1] The number four hundred also has sinister overtones for anyone with the CONTEXT TOOL to hand (1 Kings 18:19).

verses 13–16 Micaiah parodies the anti-word.
verses 17–18 Micaiah speaks the true word.
verses 19–23 Micaiah unmasks the anti-word.

Verse 13 is classic peer pressure: 'Everyone else agrees, Micaiah. They're all saying what the king wants to hear. Don't rock the boat. No need to make life difficult for yourself. Be a good chap and play along, won't you?' Brave Micaiah refuses to bend, and makes a statement that many a preacher has framed above his mantlepiece: 'As the LORD lives, what the LORD says to me, that I will speak' (verse 14).

No reader expects what happens next. Immediately after this bold declaration, Micaiah's resolve seems to crumble; he bottles it; he goes along with the crowd. Or does he? Look closely at how Micaiah's answer *functions*. What is the *effect* of Micaiah's statement?

Somehow Micaiah gets Ahab to admit to everyone that his own counsellors are lying and that he knows full well that the prophetic consensus is neither the truth nor from the LORD! We don't know exactly how Micaiah's trick worked – perhaps he used a heavily sarcastic tone or the ninth-century BC equivalent of air quotes:

> Yes, why don't you go and have your little battle. I mean, what could go wrong? It's not as if you're an evil king under a sentence of judgement from God facing a rebellion from a formidable foreign army. I'm sure you can't fail to 'win'.

And then when Ahab asks for the truth, Micaiah delivers it with both barrels:

> The truth? Forgive me, sir, I didn't think that's what you were after. The truth is that Israel will be scattered, like sheep without a shepherd. If you need me to spell out the metaphor, it means their leader snuffs it. You're going to die.

Micaiah then goes on to unmask the anti-word, as he gives us a rare glimpse into heaven, where political outcomes are *really* decided:

1 Kings 22:1–50

Down below: 'Now the king of Israel and Jehoshaphat the king of Judah were sitting on their thrones, arrayed in their robes, at the threshing floor at the entrance of the gate of Samaria, and all the prophets were prophesying before them' (verse 10).

Up above: 'I saw the LORD sitting on his throne, and all the host of heaven standing beside him on his right hand and on his left' (verse 19).

Before Ahab holds audience with various prophets, the LORD has been holding audience with various *spirits*, auditioning for someone to 'entice' the king to go to battle to meet his doom. The winning pitch comes from a 'lying spirit' who inspires the false words of Ahab's four hundred yes men.[2]

This is one of those places in Scripture that show us that while God never *does* evil (e.g., 1 John 1:5), he is nevertheless *in charge of* evil, such that it must in the end serve his own good purposes. That's true of the wicked acts of Joseph's brothers (Genesis 50:20) or the suffering inflicted by Satan on Job (Job 1:12; 2:6) or the plot against Jesus (Acts 2:23; 4:27–8).

Once again, we should reach for the AUTHOR'S PURPOSE TOOL and ask how this contributes to the overall point of the narrative: God has overseen a secret plot against Ahab, but now *tells him* about the secret plot! He permits a spirit to lie, but graciously warns Ahab that the spirit is lying. We are reminded of when Jesus cautions the Jewish leaders of his day that Satan is a 'father of lies' (John 8:44). Once you know that a particular message comes from the devil, you have no excuse for falling for it.

Ahab must now make his choice between the word he knows to be true but does not like, and the word he wants to be true but knows to be false. His first response is not encouraging. He stands

---

2 Does the role God gives to a lying spirit mean we can't always trust his word? No. God sends the deceitful spirit to work through Ahab's false prophets; there's no suggestion that any but the Holy Spirit was allowed to inspire those who wrote the Scriptures (see, for example, 2 Peter 1:21).

by as the false prophet Zedekiah 'struck Micaiah on the cheek' (verse 24) – surely a foreshadowing of the mistreatment of another servant who would speak an uncomfortable truth (John 18:22–3). Then Ahab has Micaiah thrown into prison and defies his words, predicting a safe return from the battle ('until I come in peace', verse 27).

But if Ahab has opted to trust the anti-word, why does he go to the trouble of disguising himself, while setting up gullible Jehoshaphat as the fall guy (verse 30)? If he really believes Micaiah to be false, Ahab should ride into battle leading his army. If Ahab in his heart of hearts knows Micaiah's message to be true, he should not ride into battle at all! The disguise is a pathetic attempt at fence-sitting. Throughout the chapter, Ahab tries hard to believe what he wants to believe, but never succeeds in fully convincing himself.

But while we mock Ahab, we should also look in the mirror. All of us have sometimes adopted the same strategies to avoid the truth:

- we gather a crowd of yes men
- and avoid the awkward 'Micaiah' friend
- or pressurise him to toe the line
- or marginalise him;
- we ignore the spiritual realities;
- we try to sit on the fence.

Dig deeper exercise

Use the 'SO WHAT?!' TOOL. Can you think of ways in which you have walked into a sinful situation 'in disguise'? There was something about your actions that betrayed a troubled conscience, you lacked the carefree abandon of an atheist, there was an awkwardness – but you did it anyway?

We've deliberately paused the narrative on a kind of cliff-hanger, just before the outcome of the battle at Ramoth-gilead. But honestly, it's the most predictable fall since Charlie Chaplain was filmed trying to climb the stairs. The Syrians realise Jehoshaphat is not their target (verses 31–3), but before they can even turn on their true foe, Ahab is mortally wounded by a seemingly 'random' arrow (verse 34). The battle is lost (verse 36), the king dies (verse 37) and the 'dogs licked up his blood' (verse 38), fulfilling not only Micaiah's words but also an earlier prophecy through Elijah (CONTEXT TOOL 21:19). God's word turns out to be true. The anti-word turns out to be false. Quelle surprise.

Meanwhile, in Judah …

In verses 39–50 the pace speeds up again as the author summarises what has been going on in the southern kingdom. Jehoshaphat, king of Judah, in contrast to Ahab, did 'what was right in the sight of the LORD' (verse 43). Verse 49 is a case of once bitten twice shy, as Jehoshaphat learns from the episode with Micaiah and the disastrous attack on Ramoth-gilead, and is a bit more circumspect about teaming up with his northern neighbour.

Up and down and down and up
1 Kings 22:51 – 2 Kings 1:18

Sometimes the person who put the chapter and verse numbers in the Bible (they didn't exist in the inspired original) had a bit of a bad day. But in this case they were having the worst ever day. Because not only should there not be a chapter break at the end of 1 Kings 22, but there shouldn't even be a break between 1 Kings and 2 Kings! A new section begins at 1 Kings 22:51, and then we should keep reading …

Following in the footsteps of the archetypal bad king Jeroboam, Ahaziah 'did what was evil in the sight of the LORD' (1 Kings 22:52). And like his own father, Ahab, he worshipped Baal (1 Kings 22:53). Accordingly, when he lies injured after falling through a window and needs a medical prognosis, he consults Baal-zebub, god of Ekron.[1]

The STRUCTURE TOOL and REPETITION TOOL help us appreciate the author's considerable literary craft (think John Le Carré not Dan Brown) (see Figure 8):

> **Dig deeper exercise**
> This is a chapter full of wordplay. Use the TONE AND FEEL TOOL to consider the purpose of the repeated going up and coming down (or *attempts* to get up from a sick bed and *attempts* to get Elijah down from a mountain). What is comic about it? Why do you think the author wants to make us chuckle in a passage that is in other ways quite serious?

---

1 Baalzebub may or may not be related to Beelzebul, the prince of demons referenced in Matthew 12:24.

1 Kings 22:51 – 2 Kings 1:18

Ahaziah does evil and serves Baal (22:52-3) and when injured, looks to Baal-zebub (2 Kings 1:2).

Elijah is told to **go up** and say:
> 'You shall not **come down** from the bed to which you have **gone up**, but you shall surely die' (verses 3-4).

The king's messengers report that a man **came up** and said:
> 'You shall not **come down** from the bed to which you have **gone up**, but you shall surely die' (verses 5-6).

> Ahaziah realises that the camel's-hair-clothed man was Elijah (verses 7-8)!

A captain **went up** and said to Elijah:
  'O man of God . . . **come down**!' (verse 9)
But Elijah answered
  'Let fire **come down**!'
    → fire **came down** (verse 10)
A second captain was sent to say to Elijah:
  'O man of God . . . **come down**!' (verse 11)
But Elijah answered
  'Let fire **come down**!'
    → fire of God **came down** (verse 12)
A third captain went up and pleaded with Elijah:
  'Please don't let fire **come down**!' (verses 13-14)
And the angel of the LORD told Elijah
  'It's safe to **go down**'
    → Elijah **went down** (verse 15)

Elijah says to the king
> 'You shall not **come down** from the bed to which you have **gone up**, but you shall surely die' (verse 16).
>   → he died according to the word of the LORD (verse 17).

Figure 8 **An intricate structure**

As we think further about the structure and repetition, notice how God's pronouncement of judgement comes three times:

> One. The angel tells Elijah (verses 3–4), who presumably tells the king's messengers.[2]
> Two. The king's messengers tell the king (verses 5–6).
> Three. Elijah himself tells the king, which shouldn't really be necessary because his messengers have already told him.

Notice also how a captain invites Elijah to come down from the mountain three times:

> One. Captain: 'Man of God, come down' (the fifty soldiers with him are the clue that this isn't a polite invitation to dinner). Elijah: 'Nah. Fire come down!' Even if you can't read Hebrew, you can see that the squiggles in Figure 8 look pretty similar: *ish elohim*, 'man of God', sounds almost the same as *esh elohim*, 'fire of God'[3]; by a single vowel change, Elijah vaporises them!
> Two. The king thinks better of it. Having already identified the prophet from his signature outfit (verse 8)[4] and remembered his father telling him about another incident when the true God sent fire from heaven (CONTEXT TOOL 1 Kings 18), he realises this is the time to repent. You'd think. But no. How about sending *another* captain of fifty men to insist Elijah descend from his mountaintop citadel? What could go wrong? Captain: 'Man of God, this is the king's *order*. Come down *quickly*.' Elijah: 'Nah. Fire of God come down!'
> Three. Are you ready for it? A brilliant plan. Let's send *another* captain of fifty men! It reminds us of the dedication in Terry Pratchett's novel *Guards! Guards!*

---

2 This step is omitted perhaps because for poetic reasons the author wants us to hear the message three times rather than four. It then matches the threefold visits from army captains.

3 The *ish/esh* wordplay comes throughout; in verse 12 we get the extended version, *ish elohim / esh elohim*.

4 There's actually a further joke in the Hebrew: Elijah is described as literally a 'Baal of hair', who will go head to head with Baal-zebub, 'Baal of flies'.

1 Kings 22:51 – 2 Kings 1:18

> They may be called the Palace Guard, the City Guard, or the Patrol. Whatever the name, their purpose in any work of heroic fantasy is identical: it is, round about Chapter Three (or ten minutes into the film) to rush into the room, attack the hero one at a time, and be slaughtered. No-one ever asks them if they wanted to. This book is dedicated to those fine men.[5]

Except that this third hapless captain has the sense to plead for mercy. 'Oh man of God, you've just incinerated the previous two captains with their soldiers, and it's obvious to the rest of us that it's time to repent, it's just that … well, it's not obvious to my master, see? So I was wondering if you might be willing to spare our lives, and you know, maybe instead of sending fire down, come down yourself? Just out of kindness, like?'

He receives the mercy he asks for, a wonderful reminder that God's grace remains available to any who would humble themselves.

Finally, Elijah arrives at the palace in person. With almost comic brevity the narrator shows us how utterly futile Ahaziah's mobilisation of the army against Elijah has been. The prophet merely repeats the message that has reached the king already back in verse 6, and immediately it is fulfilled. He dies (verse 17).

In fact, the story is written such that you could remove verses 5–16 and it wouldn't make any difference at all. These are entirely pointless verses. Trying to oppose God's word by a show of human strength is entirely pointless.

---

5 Terry Pratchett, *Guards! Guards!* (London: Corgi, 1990).

ELISHA

Swing low, sweet chariot
2 Kings 2

On 8 September 2022, Queen Elizabeth II died, and the crown of the United Kingdom and other Commonwealth realms passed to King Charles III. Her funeral was watched by an estimated four billion people, making it possibly the most televised event in history. King Charles' coronation in 2023 was likewise a huge occasion.

We sometimes describe succession as someone 'taking up the mantle' of their predecessor. In doing so we borrow a phrase that originated in the King James Version of 2 Kings 2:13. But while no one doubts that Charles is the rightful heir of Elizabeth, there is much more uncertainty about Elisha's candidacy at first. Elijah's successor has big shoes to fill. He will be the prophet through whom we hear the very words of God. He will be the assassin who brings an end to apostate Israel. We need to make sure we have the right guy.

As we will see shortly, the question of whether Elisha follows Elijah is bound up with whether Jesus is the true and better successor to John the Baptist. The more we grasp this chapter, the more certain we will be that Jesus is the judge of the world. Of course, you may already believe this about Jesus! But it can't hurt to have more arguments up your sleeve to silence your own doubts and to boost your evangelistic confidence.

Let's begin, as we often do, with the STRUCTURE TOOL. Tracing the geography gives us the main shape of the story:

| verse 2 | Elijah and Elisha go to *Bethel* |
| verse 4 | Elijah and Elisha go to *Jericho* |

	Elisha
verse 8	Elijah and Elisha cross the *Jordan*
verses 9–12	The handover (Elijah leaves in a whirlwind)
verse 13	Elisha crosses the *Jordan* alone
verse 15	Elisha revisits *Jericho*
verse 23	Elisha revisits *Bethel*

Even though the handover is the turning point of the story, it's not quite the turning point in the people's doubts. Their misgivings continue into the second half of the chapter, where they receive still more assurances. When they return to Jericho, we discover that Elisha can save just as Elijah did. At Bethel, we learn that he can judge just as he was appointed to do.

Elisha's quest (2 Kings 2:1–12)

It's sometimes said that the best way to test whether someone really has a calling to Christian ministry is to try to dissuade them from pursuing it. That seems to be Elijah's approach to Elisha in verses 1–7:

> Elijah: Please stay here, I'm going to Bethel.
> Elisha: As the Lord lives and as you yourself live, I will not leave you.
> [repeat x3, substituting Jericho and the Jordan as destinations]

It's like Elijah is trying to shake off an annoying puppy who refuses to let go.

At the same time, suspense mounts, as the sons of the prophets gloomily announce (twice!) Elijah's impending departure; Elisha tells them to shush.

All of this suggests doubts about Elisha, even on the part of Elijah and the faithful remnant.

The actual handover between the two prophets is then bracketed by two confirmations. In verse 9, Elisha asks for a 'double portion' (the amount due to the rightful heir, according to Deuteronomy

21:17) of Elijah's spirit. In verse 15, the sons of the prophets acknowledge that Elisha has received the same. In verse 8, Elijah strikes the Jordan River with his cloak and miraculously crosses over (for further adventures with the QUOTATION/ALLUSION TOOL see Exodus 14:21-5 and Joshua 3:14-17), and in verses 13-14 Elisha does the same.

The succession itself happens (verses 10-12), as Elisha fulfils the condition of having eyes on Elijah at the very moment of his departure (why this should be necessary, we are not told). Elijah then enjoys the almost unique privilege of ascending to heaven without having to die first.[1] It is an occasion even more spectacular than Queen Elizabeth's funeral. He leaves in a whirlwind. Chariots of fire are in attendance, inspiring a movie with the same title.

Lingering doubts dispelled (2 Kings 2:13-25)

Some of the sons of the prophets are slow to catch on to the idea that Elijah has passed on the baton, and they organise a fifty-strong search party to find him (the CONTEXT TOOL helps us discern echoes of the pointless expeditions of chapter 1). Elisha humours them but can't resist saying, 'I told you so,' when they come back empty-handed (verse 18).

The next two paragraphs bring further proof. First, just as God provided for his people miraculously through the word of Elijah, so he does the same 'according to the word that Elisha spoke' (verse 22).

Dig deeper exercise
Read 2 Kings 2:19-22.
Use the CONTEXT TOOL to remind yourself of God's prophecy concerning Elisha and his role – see 1 Kings 19:17.
Use the CONTEXT TOOL to remind yourself of God's prophecy

---

[1] If you're in a pub quiz and need to know the only other example, it's Enoch.

concerning Jericho, where Elisha's miracle occurs – see 1 Kings 16:34.

Why are Elisha's actions somewhat surprising?

It's very surprising that an assassin should bring salvation and healing to a wicked city. It's very *unsurprising* that an assassin should bring death. And for that reason, the modern reader who is outraged at the thought of bears tearing small boys into pieces after they insult a prophet for his baldness (verses 23–4) has missed the point. This takes place at Bethel, the location of one of Jeroboam I's calf-shrines, the epicentre of idolatry. A prophet of the true God arrives and is scorned. It's right that judgement should fall, and wild animal attacks were one of the curses that God promised against those who broke covenant (Leviticus 26:21–2). Our astonishment should be at God's undeserved mercy to Jericho rather than at deserved punishment at Bethel. The paradox of an assassin-saviour will be the central motif of the next six chapters.

Another succession

Two passages provide the stepping stones between 2 Kings and today. First, the prophet Malachi speaks of a future day of judgement, greater even than God's wrath against the house of Ahab:

> Behold, the day is coming, burning like an oven, when all the arrogant and all evildoers will be stubble. The day that is coming shall set them ablaze, says the LORD of hosts, so that it will leave them neither root nor branch.
> (Malachi 4:1)

But before that day comes, says Malachi, *'I will send you Elijah the prophet'* (4:5, emphasis added). So we're expecting a second 'Elijah' followed by the ultimate 'Elisha'-judge. The Elijah figure turns out to be John the Baptist. And Elisha is the Lord Jesus Christ. The fact that he has virtually the same name is the big clue: Elisha means 'God saves'; Jesus means 'Yahweh saves' (see Matthew 1:21).

The Gospel writers Matthew, Mark and Luke are all keen to drive this point home. Matthew and Mark both describe John the Baptist's clothing ('a garment of camel's hair and a leather belt around his waist', Matthew 3:4; Mark 1:6) which students of Kings immediately recognise as Elijah's signature outfit (see 2 Kings 1:8). And they both hint at parallels with 2 Kings 2 in their description of Jesus' baptism. But Luke wins the gold medal for explicit allusions (see Table 11).

John hands over to Jesus at the Jordan River (Luke 3:3).	Elijah hands over to Elisha at the Jordan River.
John the Baptist is dismayed by the apostasy of Israel and calls for their repentance (Luke 3:7–14).	Elijah is dismayed by the apostasy of Israel and calls for their repentance.
John announces that his successor (Jesus) will come to 'burn with unquenchable fire' enemies of God (Luke 3:17).	Elijah is told that his successor (Elisha) will bring judgement.
John is persecuted by Herodias, wife of King Herod (Luke 3:18–19).	Elijah is persecuted by Jezebel, wife of King Ahab.
John baptises Jesus to begin his ministry (Luke 3:21–2).	Elijah anoints Elisha to begin his ministry.
When John hands over to Jesus, heaven is opened (Luke 3:21).	When Elijah hands over to Elisha, heaven is opened.
The Holy Spirit descends on Jesus (Luke 3:22).	Elisha gets a 'double portion' of the Spirit.

Table 11 **John the Baptist and Elijah**

Jesus is a second Elisha. The 'Elijah' ministry of John the Baptist prepares the way for him. The scene is set for fire and judgement. Unexpectedly, Jesus' ministry is characterised instead by grace and salvation. But judgement will come through him in the end.

A nation saved

2 Kings 3

This chapter is one of those places where the Bible is nicely corroborated by archaeological discovery. The Moabite Stone (see Figure 9), currently on display in the Musée du Louvre, begins with the words 'I am Mesha, son of Chemosh(yat), king of Moab …' (compare verse 4) and goes on to detail Moab's military exploits against Israel after the days of Omri.[1] But let's put Scripture before the Stone and hear the divinely inspired version of events first.

Learning in verse 2 that Jehoram was not *quite* as evil as two of the most evil people in the Bible is not grounds for optimism. He is a bad king and we expect God's judgement to fall, not least because the ministry of Elisha, the bear-dispatching assassin, is underway.

The sense of foreboding increases as we discover striking parallels to the battle in 1 Kings 22 (CONTEXT TOOL) that ended in defeat. To pick up an illustration from earlier, it's like boarding a cruise ship from Southampton to New York, discovering it has been named *Titanic II*, and finding someone on board who looks like Leonardo di Caprio (see Table 12).

As we read on, things look worse and worse. After a 'circuitous march of seven days, there was no water for the army or for the animals that followed them' (verse 9). Twice (REPETITION TOOL) Jehoram cries out in panic that 'the LORD has called these three kings to give them into the hand of Moab' (verses 10, 13). The king has some understanding of God's sovereignty, but there is no evidence of him seeking God's mercy. This is fatalism rather than faith.

---

1 See the standard translation by W. F. Albright in James B. Pritchard (ed.), *Ancient Near Eastern Texts Relating to the Old Testament* (Princeton, NJ: Princeton University Press: 1969), pp. 320–21.

2 Kings 3

Figure 9 **The Moabite Stone**
(Image: public domain)

1 Kings 22	2 Kings 3
Ahab asks, 'Jehoshaphat the king of Judah' for military assistance (verse 2).	Jehoram asks, 'Jehoshaphat king of Judah' for military assistance (verse 7).
Jehoshaphat replies, 'I am as you are, my people as your people, my horses as your horses' (verse 4).	Jehoshaphat replies, 'I am as you are, my people as your people, my horses as your horses' (verse 7).
Jehoshaphat asks, 'Is there not here another prophet of the Lord of whom we may enquire?' (verse 7).	Jehoshaphat asks, 'Is there no prophet of the Lord here, through whom we may enquire of the Lord?' (verse 11).
Micaiah sought for (verses 8–9).	Elisha sought for (verses 11–12).
Micaiah prophesies defeat (verses 17–28).	. . . ?

Table 12 **Ominous parallels**

The end is nigh ... or is it?
(2 Kings 3:4–27)

Then comes a shock twist. Elisha appears, asks for musical accompaniment and delivers his message ... of salvation! This is the opposite of what the reader has been led to expect, and the opposite of what Jehoram deserves.

In fact, the LORD brings two salvations in one: a divine deluge of water prevents the army dying of thirst and – thanks to an optical illusion as the dawn's rays reflect off the surface of the water the next morning – surprise victory over the Moabites. The identification of Elisha as the one who 'poured water' over Elijah's hands seemed like a superfluous detail back in verse 11, but now, we realise, was evidence of the author's literary craft, as he subtly anticipated the miracle to come.

What an extraordinary display of grace! But we need to take care before we read it out of context. As we read on in 2 Kings, we discover that it is not salvation *instead of* judgement but salvation *before* judgement. Even within this chapter, a couple of details hint to us that the wayward nation of Israel is not off the hook:

- Just before announcing salvation, Elisha emphasises that it comes only for the sake of the king of Judah (verse 14) rather than the king of Israel. As we will be reminded later in the narrative, 'The LORD was not willing to destroy Judah, for the sake of David his servant, since he promised to give a lamp to him and to his sons forever' (8:19; compare 1 Kings 11:36; 15:4).
- Just after witnessing the salvation, the narrator tells us that 'great wrath' came against Israel, and they were forced to withdraw (verse 27).

A comment on commentaries

Instead of the usual Dig deeper exercise, we decided to devote a short section in this chapter to two difficult issues and the way they are handled in the commentaries. We shall need prayerful discernment as we weigh various interpretations in the light of the text.

Issue 1: Do Elisha's words in verse 19 violate God's law in Deuteronomy 20:19–20 (see Table 13)?

'You shall attack every fortified city and every choice city, and shall fell every good tree and stop up all springs of water and ruin every good piece of land with stones' (2 Kings 3:19).	'When you besiege a city for a long time, making war against it in order to take it, you shall not destroy its trees by wielding an axe against them. You may eat from them, but you shall not cut them down. Are the trees in the field human, that they should be besieged by you? Only the trees that you know are not trees for food you may destroy and cut down, that you may build siegeworks against the city that makes war with you, until it falls' (Deuteronomy 20:19–20).

Table 13 **Does Elisha encourage law-breaking?**

Issue 2: Whose wrath comes against Israel in verse 27? Is it the wrath of:
  a) God b) Chemosh, god of Moab c) the Moabites d) the Israelites?

One commentator answers 'no' to issue 1, because the prohibition in Deuteronomy is specific to fruit trees during sieges and so does not apply here. On issue 2, he argues for '(d) the Israelites', in the sense that the Israelites were angry *at* the child sacrifice they had witnessed. But we find that unpersuasive because the expression 'wrath against' or 'wrath upon' elsewhere in the Old Testament always refers to people suffering divine wrath, rather than feeling anger themselves.[2]

Another commentator answers '(b) Chemosh' to issue 2. That takes the biscuit. In 1 Kings 18, Baal couldn't even light a barbecue,

---

2 A similar Hebrew construction comes in Numbers 1:53; 18:5; Joshua 9:20; 1 Chronicles 27:24; 2 Chronicles 19:10; 24:18; 29:8; 32:25. Thanks to Andrew's professional Bible translator friend, Phil Reid, for extra help on this.

and in 2 Kings 1, the Baal of Ekron can't heal a broken back. So the idea that Chemosh suddenly appears on the scene to thwart God's plan is contextually unlikely, to say the least. But it does tally with the Moabites' version of events, as they claim a victory and praise Chemosh for it. 2 Kings 3:27 agrees that the Israelites had to retreat, but you could hardly describe it as a resounding Moabite win. In a masterpiece of disinformation, the Moabite Stone repeatedly boasts of 'reservoirs' that they had built, while carefully omitting any reference to the more significant pool of water that caused their downfall. The Stone doesn't refer to child sacrifice as the means by which they had tried to coax Chemosh into action,[3] perhaps again to avoid shame: even though the terrible practice was not unknown in Ancient Near Eastern religions, a king offering up the crown prince would surely have been perceived as an utterly horrifying and desperate act, even by pagan standards.[4]

Peter Leithart goes for 'Yes' and '(a) God', respectively, and connects them ingeniously as follows.[5] Elisha's words *do* contradict God's law, which seems inconceivable for God's prophet, until we take into account the parallel with 1 Kings 22, which we've already flagged with the CONTEXT TOOL (Table 12). Back then, Micaiah deliberately lied to Ahab in order to test him (1 Kings 22:15). So maybe this instruction to fell trees is a test, and the faithful king ought to realise this. But Jehoram fells the trees and thereby breaks God's law and causes Yahweh (rather than Chemosh) to be angry.

---

[3] N. T. Wright has drawn a comparison between such despicable pagan practices and some formulations of penal substitution, even borrowing Steve Chalke's notorious phrase 'cosmic child abuse', in *The Day the Revolution Began: Rethinking the meaning of Jesus's crucifixion* (San Francisco, CA: HarperOne, 2016). But when Jesus 'bore our sins in his body on the tree' (1 Peter 2:24), it was a sacrifice willed by both him and his Father: 'For this reason the Father loves me, because I lay down my life that I may take it up again. No one takes it from me, but I lay it down of my own accord. I have authority to lay it down, and I have authority to take it up again. This charge I have received from my Father' (John 10:17–18).

[4] We are grateful to George Heath-Whyte, an academic Assyriologist, for his comments on an earlier draft of this section.

[5] Peter J. Leithart, *1 & 2 Kings* (Grand Rapids, MI: Brazos Press, 2006), pp. 180–81.

Lord, spare our nation

Elisha has been named as the agent of God's judgement against an apostate people. But before judgement comes a period of salvation. How extraordinarily gracious of God!

In the chapters that follow, we will see this salvation experienced by individuals and by a particular subgroup of the population. Here it is the whole nation that is spared. It's perhaps right that we reflect on God's mercy to the United Kingdom (international readers, please feel free to substitute your own country). As a nation, we have turned our back on God our creator. Yet the peace we experience and the disasters we have escaped testify to God staying his hand of wrath.

Just across the river from London Bridge station stands a monument to the Great Fire of London (1666). The inscription it bears is a somewhat humbler reflection on a national calamity than that engraved by the Moabites:

> In the year of Christ 1666, on the 2nd September, at a distance eastward from this place of 202 feet, which is the height of this column, a fire broke out in the dead of night, which, the wind blowing devoured even distant buildings, and rushed devastating through every quarter with astonishing swiftness and noise ... Merciless to the wealth and estates of the citizens, it was harmless to their lives, so as throughout to remind us of the final destruction of the world by fire ...

A remnant saved

2 Kings 4

Variety is the spice of life. Rather than following our usual pattern of working through the passage in sections, we are going to use first the CONTEXT TOOL, then the STRUCTURE TOOL, both of which guide us to important themes we might otherwise miss. Finally, we will come to what is front and centre in the chapter: the miraculous salvation that Elisha brings.

Context: sin and judgement

The CONTEXT TOOL helps us get our bearings. Let's remind ourselves how Elisha's ministry was introduced: 'The one who escapes from the sword of Hazael shall Jehu put to death, and the one who escapes from the sword of Jehu shall Elisha put to death' (1 Kings 19:17).

His power to bring God's judgement was illustrated in the incident with the bears. Then, somewhat surprisingly, we saw him bringing salvation. But then an ominous reminder of God's wrath. We concluded that the intervention of God's grace was not salvation *instead of* judgement but salvation *before* judgement. Exile is coming. But first there is a chance to seek mercy.

Chapter 4 contains further clues that salvation is being played out against a backdrop of Israel's sin and God's judgement:

- God commanded, 'You shall not mistreat any widow or fatherless child. If you do mistreat them, and they cry out to me, I will surely hear their cry, and my wrath will burn, and I will kill you with the sword' (Exodus 22:22–4). He commanded

also, 'If your brother becomes poor beside you and sells himself to you, you shall not make him serve as a slave: he shall be with you as a hired worker and as a sojourner' (Leviticus 25:39–40). Only through flagrant disregard for God's law could the situation described in 2 Kings 4:1 arise.
- One of the curses for breaking God's covenant at Sinai was that the 'land shall not yield its increase, and the trees of the land shall not yield their fruit' (Leviticus 26:20; compare Deuteronomy 28:17–18). In 2 Kings 4:38 we read of a famine in the land.

Structure: a focus on the remnant

You may have heard of the multi-layered, Big-Mac-style, ABCBA structures in biblical writing, referred to as 'chiasms' (or sometimes, by boffins, as 'palistrophes'). We would urge caution in detecting them, because if you try hard enough you can persuade yourself that one exists almost anywhere. A silly example:

On the dining room table in front of us as we type these notes are: a bottle of water, a book of Chess openings, a pair of sunglasses, a music album, a glass. 'Knock me down with a feather, it's a CHIASM!'

Drinking vessel
    Object associated with a leisure activity
        Aid to sight
    Object associated with a leisure activity
Drinking vessel

Hopefully, we've made the point. The table does not contain a secret message from God. The chiasm exists only in our fevered imaginations. And sometimes (it seems to us) the chiasms people find in the Bible are the same, particularly those based on themes or categories chosen by the reader. However, in other cases the parallels are very specific, perhaps even using the exact same phrases, and we are persuaded that the chiasm existed in the *inspired author's* mind. Here is one such:

Salvation, by military victory, for the whole nation (3:1–27)
    Salvation for a faithful remnant, the 'sons of the prophets' (4:1–44)
        Salvation for a Gentile (5:1–27)
    Salvation for a faithful remnant, the 'sons of the prophets' (6:1–7)
Salvation, by military victory, for the whole nation (6:8 – 7:20)

Even then, this is not the last word on the structure, because the Shunammite woman, first introduced in 4:8–37, reappears in 8:1–6; sevenfold sneezes in 4:35 mirror sevenfold washings in 5:14; Naaman is leprous in 5:1 like the four men at the gate of Samaria in 7:3; the start of the conversation between Gehazi and Naaman in 5:21–2 matches exactly the conversation between Gehazi and the Shunammite in 4:26. Using the STRUCTURE TOOL is an art as well as a science: it requires judgement.

In this case, the chiasm serves to alert us to the identity of the *recipients* of God's salvation. In chapter 4 it is the faithful who are saved, and we find this highlighted in several ways:

- The phrase 'the sons of the prophets' comes three times (REPETITION TOOL verse 1, verse 38 twice); these are the same people who previously took such a keen interest in whether Elisha was legit as a successor to Elijah (see 2:5, 7, 15).
- The poor widow tells us that her late husband 'feared the LORD' (verse 1).
- The wealthy Shunammite woman goes out of her way to help Elisha, recognising him as a 'holy man of God' (verse 9) and persuading her husband to finance a loft conversion and a trip to IKEA to ensure he has comfortable accommodation (verse 10)!
- Some might think that the Shunammite's complaint in verse 28 undermines the author's emphasis elsewhere on her faithfulness. However, there is nothing unfaithful about taking a problem to the one who is able to fix it, and there are many other examples of God's people expressing themselves frankly

in moments of suffering – think Habakkuk, Job, David or even Jesus himself (e.g., Mark 15:34). Notice also how warmly Elisha responds, in contrast to the way he answers wicked Jehoram in 3:13–14.

- The sons of prophets bring the 'bread of the firstfruits' to Elisha (verse 42). This is a subtle point, but readers who have Deuteronomy 18:4–5 at their fingertips will remember that the firstfruits would ordinarily be brought to the priests. The priests in Israel were charlatans, making false sacrifices at golden calf shrines (1 Kings 12:25–33), and so the faithful remnant distance themselves from the national idolatry by going to Elisha instead. Similarly, but more subtle still, we can infer from her husband's comment in verse 23 that the Shunammite was in the habit of going to Elisha (rather than the calf shrines) for the new moon and special Sabbath festivals.

The point is clear. In a world under God's judgement, the safest place is under the shelter of the judge. Those who shun the idolatry around them and stick closely with the 'man of God' will be saved.

Elisha's power to save

Having considered the context and structure, we come finally to the main events of the chapter:

a poor widow receives miraculous oil (verses 1–7)
a rich woman receives a miraculous son twice
- he is conceived despite her infertility (verses 8–17)
- he is raised from the dead (verses 18–37)
a starving multitude are miraculously fed twice
- a deadly stew is decontaminated with flour (verses 38–41)
- a meagre amount of bread is multiplied (verses 42–4)

Given the wider context of judgement, we can characterise these as acts of 'salvation' in a broad sense. The Shunammite's experience doesn't guarantee fertility to every faithful couple struggling to conceive, just as the abundance of food for the sons of the prophets doesn't mean Christians will never go hungry. That would be to draw the lines of application too tightly. Nevertheless, we can say that God is kind to his faithful people, and will often show this in physical, practical ways (this is Jesus' point in Matthew 6:31-3).

Something more specific is going on here, though. In every episode, God's provision is clearly miraculous and – by definition – miracles are extremely rare.[1] Second, it comes through a specific man. The point is not so much that God brings salvation as that Elisha is the saviour.

The Shunammite woman realises this. When her son dies, she bizarrely reassures both her husband (verse 23) and Elisha's servant Gehazi (verse 26) that 'all is well' with him. But this pretended calmness is a strategy to meet without delay the 'man of God', on whom all her hopes are pinned.

As a miraculous saviour, Elisha is more impressive even than his predecessor, Elijah. He thus paves the way all the more clearly for his successor, Jesus.

Dig deeper exercise

Read Luke 7:11–17. Use the QUOTATION/ALLUSION TOOL. What connections can you spot with Elisha's miracle in 2 Kings 4:18–37? Be specific.

Read Luke 9:10–17. Use the QUOTATION/ALLUSION TOOL. What connections can you spot with Elisha's miracle in 2 Kings 4:42–4? For bonus points, use a Bible atlas to find out the locations of Nain and Shunem.

---

[1] Sceptics often complain that miracle claims contradict the laws of nature. In fact they depend on the universe behaving the same way 99.999% of the time, including on all the occasions when the scientists did the experiments on which the 'laws of nature' were based. If Tycho Brahe had been making his astronomical observations on the day described in 2 Kings 20:11 then Newton's law of gravity, inspired by some of Brahe's data, might have turned out a little differently. In fact the sun almost never moves that way, just as you can almost never walk on water and people almost never rise from the dead. That's why it's quite a big deal when they do.

This is what you should have found (see Table 14; we added an extra 'Elijah column' on the left as a bonus).

Elijah	Elisha (whose name means 'God saves')	Jesus (whose name means 'God saves')
Provides a miraculously bottomless jar of flour and jug of oil (1 Kings 17:8–16).	Provides a miraculously bottomless jar of oil (2 Kings 4:1–7).	Miraculously multiplies bread to feed five thousand men – in particular, he instructs his helpers to distribute a too-small amount of food, at which suggestion they are incredulous, but everyone eats, and there are leftovers (Luke 9:10–17).
	Miraculously multiplies bread to feed a hundred men – in particular, he instructs his helpers to distribute a too-small amount of food, at which suggestion they are incredulous, but everyone eats, and there are leftovers (2 Kings 4:42–4).	
Raises a widow's son from the dead, by prayer and bodily contact, in an upper room in the presence of an angry, distraught mother (1 Kings 17:17–24).	Raises a woman's son from the dead, by prayer and bodily contact, in an upper room in the presence of an angry, distraught mother (2 Kings 4:18–37).	Raises a widow's son from the dead with a word (Luke 7:11–17).

Table 14 **Miracles**

Drawing it all together

In a nation under judgement, a faithful remnant who stick close to the man of God (God's prophet, saviour and judge) will be saved.

In a world under judgement, those who stick close to Jesus (God's prophet, saviour and judge) will be saved.

A Gentile saved
2 Kings 5

We have already suggested the following macro-structure, noting the emphasis on *whom* is being saved:

Salvation, by military victory, for the whole nation (3:1–27)
   Salvation for a faithful remnant, the 'sons of the prophets' (4:1–44)
      Salvation for a Gentile (5:1–27)
   Salvation for a faithful remnant, the 'sons of the prophets' (6:1–7)
Salvation, by military victory, for the whole nation (6:8 – 7:20)

We've reached the centre of the chiasm, and the biggest surprise of all: God's mercy extends even to a Syrian, a pagan outsider, an enemy of God's people! But he is saved only as he humbles himself before the God of Israel. As such, this chapter is one of the clearest places in Scripture to understand the exclusivity *and* inclusivity of God's grace:

Salvation is inclusive
   Q: Who can be saved?
   A: Anyone, even Syrians!

Yet it is exclusive
   Q: How can Syrians be saved?
   A: Only by the God of Israel (not by Syrian gods).

In fact, only this combination of answers results in evangelism and world mission. If you're inclusively inclusive or exclusively exclusive then you won't bother.[1]

Adept users of the STRUCTURE TOOL will spot that the chapter begins with one leper (Naaman) and ends with another (Gehazi). Aside from Elisha, the Christ figure, there are in fact *three* principal characters, who all swap places in various ways:

verses 1–4	the faithful Israelite
verses 5–19a	the rich Syrian who becomes like the faithful Israelite
verses 19b–27	the faithless Israelite who becomes like the rich Syrian

The faithful Israelite (2 Kings 5:1–4)

The passage begins by introducing us to Naaman, the decorated general. Presumably he thinks that he earned all of his various medals by sheer bravery and masterful tactics and doesn't realise that (NARRATOR'S COMMENT TOOL) 'by him *the Lord had given* victory to Syria' (emphasis added). Military defeat was one of the covenant curses in threatened in Leviticus 26 and Deuteronomy 28; we are reminded yet again that God's people are under the threat of judgement.

Right at the bottom of Naaman's impressive CV, after the equivalent of 'clean driving licence', comes a detail that sets up the rest of the chapter: 'he was a leper' (verse 1). The Hebrew word doesn't refer to Hansen's disease, the neurological condition that can cause limbs to fall off, but a variety of skin conditions such as psoriasis or vitiligo. Though not life-threatening, these carry a social stigma; they also render him 'unclean' according to the law of Moses (see Leviticus 13).

However, the most important character in this first paragraph is arguably the 'little girl' (verse 2) (see Figure 10). She is the real

---

1 The inclusively inclusive viewpoint is brilliantly parodied in the poem 'Creed' by Steve Turner: 'We believe that all religions are basically the same – // at least the one we read was.' Steve Turner, *Up to Date: Poems 1968–1982* (London: Hodder and Stoughton, 1983), p. 138.

Elisha

Figure 10 **The faithful Israelite**

heroine, and it seems the author consciously holds her up as a model for his readers to follow (COPYCAT TOOL). Remember that the book of Kings ends with God's people in exile in Babylon, and part of its purpose must be to encourage them to live faithfully there. This girl, exiled to Syria, is their forerunner. And she gets everything right:

- She is faithful to God in a pagan nation, putting her trust in Elisha, the 'prophet who is in Samaria' (just like the Shunammite and the 'sons of the prophets' did back in chapter 4).
- She shows love to her enemy who has trafficked her. We might imagine her googling, 'Can leprosy be fatal?' and hoping for a positive answer. Instead, she seeks to bless him.
- She risks her life by telling him he needs the help of an Israelite prophet – the 'L' word would have been a touchy subject in Naaman's house.
- She gets the right answer to the two earlier questions. Who can be saved? Anyone, even Syrians! How can Syrians be saved? Only by the God of Israel (not by Syrian gods).

By the way, 'little girl' in Hebrew is pronounced *na'arah qetannah*. To make it masculine you take the *-ah* off the end. So 'little boy' is *na'ar qaton*. More on this later …

The rich Syrian who becomes like the faithful Israelite (2 Kings 5:5–19)

Naaman starts off entirely on the wrong foot, which introduces some great comedy. Instead of listening carefully to the little girl's instructions to consult 'the prophet in Samaria', he gets his master to write to the king of Israel. 'I'm important,' he thinks to himself. 'I'll pull some strings and go straight to the top.' At which point King Joram panics, assuming he's been asked to do the impossible by a hostile foreign power, to sour diplomatic relations as a pretext for war. 'Am I God, to kill and to make alive?' he cries (verse 7) – a moment of rare humility from a wicked royal family who have acted repeatedly as though they were indeed in the place of God.

When Naaman eventually reaches Elisha, carrying 'ten talents of silver, six thousand shekels of gold' and ten Armani suits – he's expecting Harley Street[2] prices – he again shows a reluctance to follow simple instructions. 'I'm important,' he thinks to himself.

> I thought that he would surely come out to me [he's incensed that Elisha doesn't even answer the door himself] and stand and call upon the name of the Lord his God, and wave his hand over the place [surely the job of the priest is to produce a convincing religious spectacle?] and cure the leper. Are not Abana and Pharpar, the rivers of Damascus, better than all the waters of Israel? Could I not wash in them and be clean? [Are you suggesting I need a bath? How dare you! Besides, my river's better than your river and my god's better than your God!]
> (2 Kings 5:11-12)

It's our heroine's fellow-servants who talk sense into him (verse 13), and he humbles himself and washes and is healed.

When reading biblical narrative, we need to travel at different speeds. Sometimes, we can drive along at 40mph, following the

---

2 For international readers, Harley Street is home to some of the best and most expensive medical practitioners in London.

storyline and admiring the view (as we've just done in verses 5–13). When it comes to verse 14, we suggest putting on the handbrake, turning off the engine and getting out of the car. This is a verse full of theology, and the details matter.

We have seen that when the author of 1 – 2 Kings wants to celebrate a fulfilled prophecy, he describes the prophecy and its fulfilment in exactly the same words. For instance, if we had been told, 'He will eat an orange, and the juice will squirt out and it will stain his shirt,' we then expect to read, 'He ate an orange, and the juice squirted out and it stained his shirt, according to the word that the LORD had spoken.' For actual biblical examples see 1 Kings 17:14 (with verse 16); 2 Kings 3:19 (with verse 25); 4:43 (with 4:44).

At this point we have set you up for the big reveal and, with considerable self-restraint, will let you discover it for yourself (Alasdair literally had to prise the keyboard out of Andrew's hands to prevent him from telling you).

> **Dig deeper exercise**
>
> Use the PARALLELS TOOL to set verse 10 alongside verse 14. How do the prophecy and fulfilment line up when put next to each other? What is the same?
> What extra phrase has the author added, breaking with convention?
> Why is this a big deal (hint: guess the words in the original Hebrew)?

In Hebrew, it says Naaman's flesh is restored like a *na'ar qaton*! Remember that phrase? The rich Syrian has become like the faithful Israelite (see Figure 11).[3]

Once we spot this, it opens up a world of transformations:

- The little girl, though in Syria, believed in the God of Israel (verse 3). Now Naaman, a Syrian, exclaims, 'There is no god

---

[3] We were first alerted to this by Walter Brueggemann, *1 & 2 Kings* (Macon: Smyth & Helwys, 2000), p. 334, who observes that 'the girl is presented . . . as an innocent, trusting, whole person, as an earnest of what the general will become through the ministration of Elijsha. The healed "flesh" of the general is like the flesh of the young, perhaps the very young, thus "baby flesh."'

2 Kings 5

Figure 11 **The rich Syrian becomes like the faithful Israelite**

in all the earth but in Israel' (verse 15). Who can be saved? Anyone, even Syrians! How can Syrians be saved? Only by the God of Israel (not by Syrian gods).

- In Syria, the little girl is far from her true home in Israel. But verse 17 (have a look) suggests that Naaman, on his return, will feel the same. We use the expression 'on British soil' to refer metaphorically or legally to British embassies abroad, but he takes the concept quite literally! He now belongs among the people of God, and returning 'home' will feel like living as an exile.[4]
- The little girl must have felt awkward about the pagan practices around her. Naaman, on his return, will feel the same. His conscience sits uneasily with the thought of attending state occasions in the temple of the fake-god Rimmon, and he asks for the Lord's pardon when he bows down there. Bruce Waltke explains a delicious joke in the original: the god's name was in fact Ramanu, meaning 'storm god,' and Naaman has deliberately changed the pronunciation so that it means 'when I bow before the pomegranate'.[5] He no longer respects his pagan past.

---

4 Compare the description of Christians as 'exiles' or 'sojourners' (1 Peter 1:1).
5 Bruce K. Waltke, *An Old Testament Theology: An exegetical, canonical, and thematic approach* (Grand Rapids, MI: Zondervan, 2011), p. 728.

How the LORD has changed Naaman! Not only is his leprosy gone, but also his pride and his paganism.

The faithless Israelite who becomes like the Rich Syrian (2 Kings 5:20–27)

Whereas the prophet made no profit, Gehazi decides to cash in. He chases after Naaman and tells him a pack of lies, as a result of which he heads home with two talents of silver and two designer outfits. Naaman's cheerful giving (twice the amount of silver that Gehazi asks for) to support, as he is led to believe, 'two young men of the sons of the prophets' (verse 22) serves to demonstrate his new solidarity with the faithful remnant, even as it betrays Gehazi's wickedness.

Unfortunately for Gehazi, everything was caught on Elisha's prophetic CCTV (verses 25–6). A terrible sentence is pronounced: 'the leprosy of Naaman shall cling to you and to your descendants for ever' (verse 27). Thus the faithless Israelite becomes like the rich Syrian (see Figure 12).

What is it about Gehazi that causes him to lose everything? His greed? Perhaps. His disregard for truth? Possibly. But Elisha's judgement begins with a question: 'Was it a time to accept money and garments …?' There is nothing wrong with plundering an

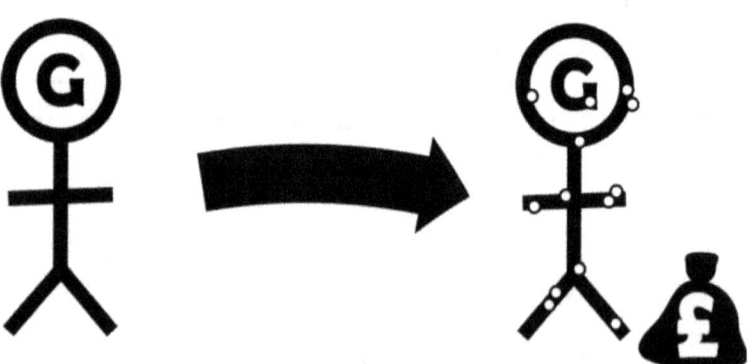

Figure 12 **The faithless Israelite becomes like the rich Syrian**

enemy, and in a couple of chapters we will read of lepers(!) gleefully pillaging the Syrian camp. But now *is not the time*, because Naaman is no longer an enemy. Gehazi has just witnessed one of the great biblical demonstrations that God can save anyone,[6] and he should be embracing him as a brother. Instead, he speaks of 'this Naaman the Syrian' (verse 20) with evident disdain.

Inclusively exclusive

The first readers of 1 - 2 Kings, in exile in Babylon, would have been tempted to either syncretism – amalgamating the beliefs of the culture around them – or xenophobia – barricading themselves from the outside world. The glorious story of Naaman's conversion encourages them to take neither path. Like the little girl (and unlike Gehazi), they must hold on to the twin convictions that a) only the true God can save, and b) he can save anyone.

Jesus alluded to the story of Naaman in Luke 4:27, to explain that as Israel rejects God, he is more than willing to bless the foreigner instead. The Pharisees respond with Gehazi-like rage. But the faithful Christian should respond with joy, realising that the exclusive gospel of salvation only through Jesus (Acts 4:12) is intended, inclusively, for all nations (see Luke 2:32 and 24:47, bracketing Luke's Gospel; Acts 1:8 and 28:28, bracketing the book of Acts).

Who is the 'little girl' today? She is the lone Christian in the office, who pipes up to tell her atheist CEO, 'If only my master would go to the Lord Jesus [the greater Elisha]; he would cure him of his sin [the greater leprosy].'

Who is the Gehazi today? He lives in an exclusive religious ghetto, trying his best to keep everyone else out.

---

[6] Others include Jesus talking to a Samaritan at a well (John 4); Jesus agreeing to give 'crumbs' to a Syrophoenician woman (Mark 7); Peter eating with Cornelius after receiving a vision of a sheet descending from heaven full of delicious but 'unclean' foods (Acts 10).

Blindness and sight

2 Kings 6:1 – 8:6

Help for the godly but clumsy (2 Kings 6:1–7)

> **Dig deeper exercise**
> Read 2 Kings 6:1–7. Use the AUTHOR'S PURPOSE TOOL. Why is it important for us to know how the prophet miraculously intervenes to spare a faithful Israelite (he's a goodie, one of the 'sons of the prophets') from exorbitant late-return fees at the Tool Hire shop?
> Leithart suggests that the axe head, seeing as it's made of wood, foreshadows the salvation that comes through the cross; and that because it descends into water before rising again, it may symbolize Christian baptism.[1] Are you persuaded?
> How would you fit this episode into the bigger picture that the author is painting?

Eyes open; eyes closed (2 Kings 6:8–23)

In Paul's first prayer for the Ephesians, he prays that God would open their spiritual eyes (Ephesians 1:18). Jesus famously opens the eyes of the blind, physically (e.g., Luke 7:22; 18:42). On the road to Damascus, Jesus blinds Saul (Acts 9:8–9).

Opening spiritual eyes. Closing physical eyes. Opening physical eyes. In this chapter God does all three.

---

1 Peter J. Leithart, *1 & 2 Kings* (Grand Rapids, MI: Brazos Press, 2006), pp. 200–01.

It appears that the king of Syria is just as stupid as Ahaziah was back in chapter 1. Even though his own advisers tell him that Elisha has him under a level of intelligence coverage that would make MI6 proud (verse 12), he imagines he can seize the man of God by brute force and sends a vast army of horses and chariots to encircle the city (verses 13-14). What he doesn't know, and Elisha's servant doesn't know either until his spiritual eyes are opened (verses 16-17), is that the vast army is surrounded by an even vaster army of horses and chariots *of fire*. Being a dad, it reminds me (Alasdair) of the classic cartoon fish chase sequence, where an average sized fish is about to eat a tiny fish, oblivious to the enormous fish coming up behind it.[2]

Having prayed that God would improve his servant's spiritual surveillance capabilities, Elisha then asks God to disrupt the enemies' physical ones. This isn't a case of jamming the radar or shooting down the reconnaissance drone. God strikes them blind so they can't even see their hands in front of their face.

There is a further surprise in this section. Not only does God save Elisha from the Syrians, but he *saves the Syrians from Israel*. This is extraordinary grace. Someone might point out that the law prescribed as much, in its regulations concerning prisoners of war (Deuteronomy 20:10-15), but this only reinforces the point: God's law is extraordinarily gracious! In fact, Elisha asks them to go further and treat the Syrians to a banquet before sending them home!

Yet another undeserved victory (2 Kings 6:24 – 7:20)

The assurance that 'the Syrians did not come again on raids into the land of Israel' (verse 23) does not mean the end of hostilities altogether. Instead, what follows is a full-blown invasion (verse 24).

The ensuing siege brings terrible hardship. Tiny amounts of poor-quality food and fuel sell for massively inflated prices (verse 25), and the hunger is so bad that a woman will even eat her own

---

[2] The chariots of fire also remind us of Elijah's welcome party when he ascended into heaven in 2:11-12 (CONTEXT TOOL).

child. The story is horrific enough on its own, but with the QUOTATION/ALLUSION TOOL we recall that cannibalism was a specific curse on those who broke God's covenant (Deuteronomy 28:53–7). We may also discern a twisted echo of the story of Solomon and two women arguing over a baby (1 Kings 3:16–28).

The king's despair in verse 30 makes sense, but not his desire to kill Elisha in verse 31. For one thing, it won't work – Ahaziah failed spectacularly in his efforts to bump off Elijah back in 2 Kings 1. But why would you even *want* to snuff out your only hope of salvation? In an act of defiant theological self-harm, he would rather curse the saviour than seek mercy.

However, when he sends armed guards to murder Elisha, Elisha prophesies that God will save them from the siege (6:32 – 7:2). The prophecy is then fulfilled exactly, to an almost pedantic level of detail (see Table 15).

'Elisha said . . . "Tomorrow about this time a seah of fine flour shall be sold for a shekel, and two seahs of barley for a shekel"' (7:1).	'So a seah of fine flour was sold for a shekel, and two seahs of barley for a shekel, according to the word of the LORD' (7:16).
'The captain . . . said to the man of God, "If the LORD himself should make windows in heaven, could this thing be?" But he said, "You shall see it with your own eyes, but you shall not eat of it"' (7:2).	The faithless captain is trampled to death by the stampede of people rushing to buy the abundant food at bargain prices, and so doesn't get to eat of it himself (7:20).

Table 15 **Bargain prices!**

Yet the king does not at first believe it (verses 12–15). It is outsiders, the lepers, who first find out about the miraculous salvation of the city (verses 3–11). The CONTEXT TOOL reminds us of another leper, Naaman, and we notice that while it was not the time in 5:26 to take things from Syrians when Naaman came in humility, it is the time to plunder them in 7:16 when Ben-hadad comes in conquest.

Once again, hostility to God is met with undeserved grace in another example of salvation for the whole nation. It is a kind of mirror image of chapter 3:

In one, an army leaves a city expecting to find an empty camp and is surprised to find an army; in the second, lepers leave a city expecting to find a full camp and are surprised to find an empty camp.[3]

God doesn't do coincidences (2 Kings 8:1–6)

After five chapters of salvation (arranged in a Big Mac shape, as we've seen) judgement is about to fall. But first, one last celebration of the *'great things that Elisha has done'* (verse 4, emphasis added), as the exploits are regaled to the king. Three curious features stand out:

First, the narrator is Gehazi. Remember him? He serves as a living, walking reminder of both God's judgement (in the case of his own leprosy) and God's unexpected mercy to Naaman.

Second, the whole episode is taken out of chronological order. The seven-year gap mentioned in verse 3 places the episode in the reign of Jehu, who won't become king until the next chapter! The author is keen to bring this bit of good news forward.

Third, by a staggering (surely providential) coincidence, at the very moment that Gehazi is telling the king about the resurrection of the Shunammite's son, who should walk in the door but the woman herself (verse 5)!

Why this cameo from the Shunammite? Grace has repeatedly been shown to an idolatrous king and people, and yet, as it comes to a close, we still see no signs of real, lasting repentance. The window of opportunity has come and gone, and we are about to see judgement unfold in a horrifying way. Yet as we teeter on the brink, the author reminds us one last time of the God who raised up a saviour. Could there be another Elisha to come?

---

3 Peter J. Leithart, *1 & 2 Kings* (Grand Rapids, MI: Brazos Press, 2006), p. 206.

God's assassins
2 Kings 8:7 – 10:31

Andrew went to see *Oppenheimer*, the multi-Oscar-winning Christopher Nolan film, with a good friend and his younger son, who had assured him that it carried a PG certificate. In fact, it's a fifteen certificate – and with good reason: it features a fairly explicit sex scene and graphic depictions of the effects of a nuclear blast on the human body. The son – who had made an honest mistake about the rating – was mortified and spent much of the movie with his hoodie pulled down over his face.

You'd hesitate to take even an eighteen-year-old to the film of 2 Kings 8 – 10. It's gory and relentlessly brutal. Many people would be shocked to discover it's in the Bible at all. The assassins for whom we've been waiting since 1 Kings 19:15–17 finally arrive. None of God's enemies is left alive.

Prologue (2 Kings 8:7 – 9:13)

Shakespeare might easily have got the idea for Macbeth from these first few verses (8:7–15). When consulted by Hazael about Benhadad's medical prognosis (incidentally, it's ironic that the pagan goes to God's prophet, where the king of Israel consulted Baalzebub; compare 1:2), Elisha answers in what seems to the reader a strange paradox: "'You shall certainly recover', … he shall certainly die', verse 10). But Hazael's embarrassment at the fixed stare that accompanies the prediction suggests he understands entirely. His master will recover from illness but die by the hand of Hazael himself. He denies it (verse 13), but by the end of the paragraph the deed is done and he is king of Syria.

It is worth pausing to consider Elisha's tears (verse 11). It makes us think of Jesus weeping over Jerusalem (Luke 19:41), or the Apostle Paul's tears at the coming destruction of the wicked (Philippians 3:18). The judgement which Hazael will bring is right and God-ordained, but *at the same time* sad and terrible.

The next paragraph (8:16–29) prepares the reader for the scope of Jehu's judgement, extending beyond Israel to include two wayward kings of Judah.

> **Dig deeper exercise**
>
> For the most part, Judah's kings have been the good guys (for a recent example, see 3:14). But now we learn that Jehoram and his son Ahaziah have gone wrong.
>
> Read 2 Kings 8:18. Use the LINKING WORDS TOOL. What's the reason that Jehoram went astray?
>
> Read 2 Kings 8:27. Use the LINKING WORDS TOOL. What's the reason that Ahaziah went astray?

Not for the first time in 1 – 2 Kings, marrying an unbeliever brings disaster. Judah is in bed with Israel, literally and metaphorically, and is about to share in her fate. Yet God has not forgotten David, and for the third time in the book we are reminded that he 'promised to give a lamp to him and to his sons forever' (verse 19; see also 1 Kings 11:36; 15:4).

Let's return to the main story, though, concerning the northern tribes of Israel. We are preparing for judgement. It's a double-barrelled shotgun, and Elisha has already loaded the Hazael chamber. Now, in 9:1–13, Jehu is anointed and the second chamber is loaded. The author emphasises that this is ultimately God's doing: 'Thus says the LORD, the God of Israel, I anoint you king over Israel' (REPETITION TOOL, verses 3, 6, 12).

Jehu on the warpath (2 Kings 9:14 – 10:27)

We thought the best way to describe Jehu's blood-soaked rampage was in a table (see Table 16), the better to bring out the recurring

Elisha

	Memorable details	RECURRING THEME: Apostates change sides to join Jehu's 'remnant'	RECURRING THEME: God's word fulfilled
Joram and Ahaziah killed (9:14-29)	The REPETITION TOOL reveals Joram's desperate but futile search for reassurance: 'Is it peace?' (verses 17, 18, 19, 22). Jehu's answer comes in verse 22: there can be no peace where there is spiritual adultery.	Joram's messengers on horseback now ride behind Jehu (verses 18-20).	In 1 Kings 21:17-24, Elijah promised that Ahab would be killed at the vineyard of Naboth, his victim, and that all his male descendants would be 'cut off'. Elisha reminded Jehu of this in 2 Kings 9:7-8, and now he orders that Joram be killed in the same place as his father 'in accordance with the word of the LORD' (2 Kings 9:25-6).
Jezebel killed (9:30-37)	Echoing her son, Jezebel asks, 'Is it peace?', but from her reference to Zimri (compare 1 Kings 16:9-20), we infer she knows otherwise. She beautifies herself (verse 30), but soon all that's left of her is 'the skull and the feet and the palms of her hands' (verse 35); even the fingers have been chewed off by dogs.	Two or three eunuchs from Jezebel's household, throw her out the window in response to Jehu's cry, 'Who is on my side? Who?' (verses 32-3). The uncertainty about the precise number suggests an eyewitness report from someone in the courtyard who couldn't quite see!	In 1 Kings 21:23, the LORD said, 'The dogs shall eat Jezebel within the walls of Jezreel'. They do. Interestingly, it seems that Jehu has forgotten this prophecy and orders her burial, but God arranges events so his word comes to pass instead (2 Kings 9:34-7).
Ahab's other sons killed (10:1-17)	The graphic image of heads shipped in baskets (verse 7) and piled high either side of the city gate (verse 8) is surely intended to lodge in our minds. The REPETITION TOOL shows the author's emphasis on the totality of the judgement: '*all* who remained . . . *none* remaining . . . he spared *none* of them . . . *all* who remained' (verses 11, 14, 17, emphasis added).	The 'rulers of the city . . . the elders . . . the guardians of the sons of Ahab' (verse 1) surrender to Jehu: 'We are your servants, and we will do all that you tell us' (verse 5). In response to his command, they assassinate their wards, and he pronounces them 'innocent' (verse 9). It seems Jehu then spares them when he kills a different group, those 'who remained of the house of Ahab . . . all his great men and his close friends and his priests' (verse 11).	Jehu 'struck down all who remained to Ahab in Samaria, till he had wiped them out, according to the word of the LORD that he spoke to Elijah' (verse 17).

Table 16 **Jehu on the rampage**

	Memorable details	RECURRING THEME: Apostates change sides to join Jehu's 'remnant'	RECURRING THEME: God's word fulfilled
Prophets of Baal killed (10:18–27)	Through the pretence of hosting a 'solemn assembly to Baal' (verse 20), Jehu successfully gathers the apostate priests. Brilliantly, he then gives *them* the task of ensuring no troublesome 'servant of the LORD' has infiltrated the gathering (verse 23), before unleashing his eighty assassins (verses 24–5). As above, the REPETITION TOOL shows the emphasis on the totality of the judgement: 'all the prophets of Baal, all his worshippers and all his priests. Let none be missing' (verse 18); 'the house of Baal was filled' (verse 21); 'all the worshippers of Baal' (verse 22). The author saves the best detail until last: they turn Baal's temple into a toilet (verse 27).	Jehonadab is a little different. From the start his heart is true to Jehu (verse 15), and he co-orchestrates the plot against the prophets of Baal. (He is commended at length in Jeremiah 35!)	

Table 16 **Jehu on the rampage** (*continued*)

features. In each narrative the author shares graphic details that stick in the mind, and presumably are intended to (TONE AND FEEL TOOL). In each we find people changing sides to join Jehu, and thereby sparing their own lives – perhaps sheer pragmatism or perhaps genuine repentance. In each we find the fulfilment of prophecy underlining that, for all his brutality, Jehu's actions are in line with God's plan.

A quick aside on dates: does Ahaziah become king in the 'twelfth year of Joram' (8:25) or the 'eleventh year of Joram' (9:29)? This is exactly the kind of issue that we expect a good commentary to help us with, and Iain Provan comes up trumps. He explains that a year's discrepancy can be 'resolved easily at one level by accepting that dates could be reckoned in different ways, particularly in the way that partial years were handled'.[1] In other words, it's a case of rounding up and rounding down. In 9:29 we need to round down to fit in a one-year reign for Ahaziah before he is killed at the same time as Joram.

Theological evaluation of Jehu and Hazael (2 Kings 10:28–36)

Instinctively we condemn Jehu; we say he's gone too far; we distance ourselves. The inspired author thinks differently. He condemns Jehu for the calf-idolatry that he left unchecked (verses 29, 31), but *not* for his bloody executions. In fact, he records a specific word of the LORD that may shock us: 'You have done well in carrying out what is right in my eyes, and have done to the house of Ahab according to all that was in my heart' (verse 30).

This is a very high level of commendation: the phrase 'right in my eyes' is otherwise used in 1 – 2 Kings only for David and the good kings of *Judah* (1 Kings 15:5, 22:43; 2 Kings 12:2; 14:3, etc.).

For those troubled by Hosea 1:4, Duane Garrett helpfully explains:

> It should be translated, 'I will bring the bloodshed of Jezreel on the house of Jehu.' This is not punishment for Jehu's zeal for the slaughter at Jezreel; rather it is punishment for not learning the lesson of Jezreel. Jehu himself had been the agent of God's fury and personally had seen how terribly it fell upon an apostate dynasty. But he and his household went on to repeat the apostasy.[2]

The focus of these chapters has been on Jehu, but his actions are framed by mentions of the parallel campaign of Hazael (9:14–15;

---

1 Iain W. Provan, *1 & 2 Kings* (Grand Rapids, MI: Baker Books, 1995), p. 213.
2 Duane A. Garrett, *Hosea, Joel: The New American Commentary* (Nashville, TN: B&H, 1998), p. 57.

10:32). To return to our shotgun analogy, the LORD has fired at Israel with both barrels.

The Lord Jehu Christ?

We've seen repeatedly that apostasy brings judgement. But now we see God's wrath poured out on a bigger and more terrifying scale. It will escalate further, of course, for even the terror of Jehu does not compare with the horrors of Assyrian and Babylonian invasions.

In the previous few chapters, we have celebrated Elisha as a type of Christ. He was expected as a judge but came first to offer salvation.

Jehu is also a type of Christ. Uniquely among the kings of the northern kingdom, he is a 'messiah', i.e., a king anointed by a prophet of the LORD (9:6). He is described as having 'zeal for the LORD' (10:16); and he shares with only one other person the distinction of having cloaks thrown down to pave the way for his coronation (9:13; compare Luke 19:36).

Does it shock us to think of Jesus in this way? Are you squeamish at the idea of his brutal destruction of the wicked? We admit that we can be, sometimes. And yet the prophecies about him at the end of the Bible make Jehu look tame:

> Then I saw heaven opened, and behold, a white horse! The one sitting on it is called Faithful and True, and in righteousness he judges and makes war. His eyes are like a flame of fire, and on his head are many diadems, and he has a name written that no one knows but himself. He is clothed in a robe dipped in blood, and the name by which he is called is The Word of God. And the armies of heaven, arrayed in fine linen, white and pure, were following him on white horses. From his mouth comes a sharp sword with which to strike down the nations, and he will rule them with a rod of iron. He will tread the wine press of the fury of the wrath of God the Almighty. On his robe and on his thigh he has a name written, King of kings and Lord of lords.
> (Revelation 19:11–16)

THE DOWNWARD SPIRAL

The house in the house
2 Kings 11 – 12

Something is different. The landscape has altered. There are references to the house of the LORD, the Sabbath, priests of the LORD, and 'spears and shields that had been King David's' (11:10). If you haven't worked it out yet: we are back in Judah.

We shouldn't underestimate the significance of this shift in location. Recall that after the apostasy of Solomon in 1 Kings 11, the kingdom was torn in two, and ever since 1 Kings 15:21 we have been tracing the history of the northern tribes and their kings, who almost invariably followed in the footsteps of 'Jeroboam son of Nebat' who 'made Israel to sin'. There have been some references to the kings of Judah, but only where their storylines intersected with that of the northern kingdom – such as when the numpty Jehoshaphat went into battle with the house of Ahab (twice), or when Ahaziah tragically married into Ahab's wicked family.

The theologically informed reader is especially concerned about Judah because of the king in the line of David and because of the Temple – the two inextricably linked by the famous wordplay in 2 Samuel 7, when God spoke of both a house (dynasty) and a house (temple).

All of this is in our minds as the camera crew heads south to document the story of Jerusalem, Joash, Jehosheba and Jehoiada. The account splits into two parts:

11:1–20	Joash protected and crowned in the Temple.
11:21 – 12:21	Joash refurbishes the Temple.

The house of God protects the house of David (2 Kings 11:1–20)

Like his forefathers David (who contended with Ish-bosheth) and Solomon (versus Adonijah), Joash's succession to the throne is opposed by a dangerous rival. In this case it's his evil grandmother, Athaliah, who bears more than a passing resemblance to Jezebel, the arch-villain. In fact, she may even be her daughter, given that Ahab, Jezebel's husband, was her father (2 Kings 8:18). Athaliah goes about eliminating the true heirs to the throne (verse 1) and seizes it for herself (verse 3). Her reign is so illegitimate that the author refuses to dignify it with the summary formula that closes the account of every other monarch in the book. Nonetheless, for six terrible years, Athaliah holds sway.

Humanly speaking, it is faithful Auntie Jehosheba and her husband Jehoiada who save the day. We will trace their strategy first and then consider evidence of God's hand of Providence at work.

A strategy for survival

Step one is Jehosheba hiding Joash 'in the house of the LORD' (verse 3). This is a great choice for a hideaway or safe house, because Athaliah was descended from Baal worshippers. You would be more likely to find Greta Thunberg at a Monster Truck Rally than idolatrous Athaliah at the Temple of the true and living God. Young Joash remains there in secret for the next six years.

Next, Jehoiada repositions the royal guard. The specific details are complicated, but the basic point is that those previously guarding the royal palace (Athaliah) now guard the Temple (Joash). That much is clear from verses 7–8. We struggled with verse 6 in the ESV because some guards move from the 'king's house' to the 'palace', which is surely the same place?! The translators admit, in the footnote, that 'the meaning of the Hebrew word is uncertain.' Provan suggests it should be translated 'house of destruction', referring to the house of Baal which is later destroyed (verse

18).¹ If he's right, that means that the guard is split between defence of the true Temple and attack (or at least preparation for attack) on the false one.

Then, with his well-armed muscle stationed and ready in the best tactical locations, Jehoiada places the crown on Joash's head and, significantly, gives him the 'testimony' – the word refers to the two stone tablets inscribed with the Ten Commandments. This is presumably a *copy*, the original being kept inside the ark of the covenant in the Temple (see, for example, Exodus 25:16). It is exactly the right thing to do. Deuteronomy 17:18–20 instructed the king to make a copy of the law for himself in order that:

> … he shall read it in all the days of his life, that he may learn to fear the LORD his God by keeping all the words of this law and these statutes, and doing them, that his heart may not be lifted up above his brothers, and that he may not turn aside from the commandment, either to the right hand or to the left, so that he may continue long in the kingdom, he and his children, in Israel.

Jehoiada takes no chances, and does the legwork himself, presenting the king with a version already copied out. It reminds us of the faithful godparent who sends Bible-reading notes to his teenage godson, as a kind of nudge to get stuck into God's word. Given that Joash's father and grandfather 'walked in the way of the house of Ahab' (8:27; compare 8:18), it is crucial that this young king reverts to the ways of his great-great-great-great-great-great-grandfather, David.

Next, Jehoiada executes the pretender to the throne. Hearing the joyful sounds of clapping and trumpets (reminiscent of the coronations of Solomon and Jehu), Athaliah enters the Temple to see what is going on, discovers the coronation and cries, 'Treason!' A tad hypocritical, considering her own route to power. She is summarily executed (verse 16).

---

1 Iain W. Provan, *1 & 2 Kings* (Grand Rapids, MI: Baker Books, 1995). p. 222.

The downward spiral

Then Jehoiada 'made a covenant between the LORD and the king and the people, that they should be the LORD's people, and also between the king and the people' (verse 17). It's like the Magna Carta, except not only is the king promising to relate rightly to the people, but they are also both promising to relate rightly to God. As a direct consequence of this, it seems, they all march to the temple of Baal to tear it down, and to kill Mattan, the priest of Baal (verse 18), echoing the actions of Elijah (1 Kings 18) and Jehu (2 Kings 10) in the northern kingdom. The rejection of false worship is also subtly underlined in the comparison between verses 15 and 18: the Temple of the LORD is too holy to witness an execution, whereas desecrating the temple of Baal with the corpse of a false priest is fair game.

Finally, Jehoiada orchestrates a royal procession that ends with Joash taking 'his seat on the throne of the kings' (verse 19). The summary in verse 20 is instructive: the false queen is deposed, the Davidic king is seated, and 'the city was quiet'. Peace at last.

So, in summary, Jehoiada (a) hides Joash, (b) gets him safely crowned, (c) hands him some Bible-reading notes, (d) executes the godless Athaliah, (e) makes a covenant that the people should be God's people, (f) oversees the destruction of Baal-worship, (g) has the king enthroned, and (h) brings about a 'quiet' city.

Dig deeper exercise

The ESV reads as follows for 12:2: 'Jehoash did what was right in the eyes of the LORD all his days, because Jehoiada the priest instructed him.'

Use the TRANSLATIONS TOOL to compare how the NIV renders the verse: 'Joash did what was right in the eyes of the LORD all the years Jehoiada the priest instructed him.'

Can you spot the subtle difference in the meaning? Do you detect an ominous note?

Read 2 Chronicles 24:17–18. How does this support the NIV interpretation?

Pray for churches where a faithful minister is about to retire, that they would not lack for biblical instruction in the future.

God ensures his promises stay on track

So is Jehoiada the sole hero of the story? Is he the one responsible for everything that goes right, with the help of his sidekick Jehosheba and the loyal guards? When we put on our theological spectacles, we see that God is the one ultimately at work *through* Jehoiada and Jehosheba. It is not obvious at first, because (unlike many other places in 1 – 2 Kings) God's agency is not mentioned explicitly. But we discern his hand because of the house and the house.

The LORD promised to preserve the house of David. Jehoiada's actions are the means by which that word is fulfilled.

And the house of David is preserved in the 'house of the LORD' (mentioned no fewer than twenty-two times in these two chapters, REPETITION TOOL), and it has significance theologically beyond being a shrewd hiding place. This was the place where the cloud of God's glory had descended to be with his people (1 Kings 8:10–11), just as it had done on Mount Sinai (Exodus 20) and on the tabernacle in the wilderness (Exodus 40:34–8). It represents God's presence with his people. Note also how our hero Jehoiada is connected intimately with this place: he is a *priest*. Lissa M. Wray Beal puts it this way:

> The coup is solely directed by the priest, and derives its moral and theological power from the sacred space of the temple. In it the king is reinstalled and acknowledged, and covenants are reforged. Athaliah is escorted from the sacred space so that her death should not mar it. When the king ascends the palace throne after the false cult is deposed, he extends the temple's holy reach to that civic space. Finally, the people's rejoicing and the quieted land evidence the extension of the temple's holiness further outwards to the people and land.[2]

In the way this dramatic story of Athaliah the usurper and her sticky end is told, we learn that God's 2 Samuel 7 promise will come to pass no matter what obstacles get in the way.

---

2 Lissa M. Wray Beal, *1 & 2 Kings* (Nottingham: Apollos, 2014), p. 392.

Joash refurbishes the Temple (2 Kings 11:21 – 12:21)

Having appreciated the centrality of the house of God in these chapters, there is then both encouragement and disappointment in the description of the work done to refurbish it.

Encouraging signs include the following:

- People made donations of their own free will (verse 4) to have the Temple repaired (compare Exodus 35:20–9).
- Care was taken to ensure transparency in the handling of the money (verses 9–10). Jehoiada comes up with the concept of a collection box, where anyone can stick a ten-pound note in the hole in the top, but only authorised people can take the money out the bottom. And he specified that there should be *two* authorised people – even a godly priest shouldn't be trusted to count the money on his own. There's much wisdom here for our churches. The Jehoiada system of financial accounting would avoid many a scandal.
- The workmen were honest, to such an extent that they did not need to appoint auditors (verse 15)!

But there are major discouragements too:

- The priests sat on the funds for twenty-three years (verse 6) without making any repairs.
- The donations were sufficient only to pay for labour and materials (verses 11–12) and to give a living to the priests (verse 16), but not to replace some of the Temple inventory (verse 13).
- More Temple treasures were given to Hazael king of Syria (verses 17–18). This reminds us (CONTEXT TOOL) of the time when Rehoboam and Asa gave Temple treasures away to Shishak, king of Egypt (1 Kings 14:26) and Ben-hadad king of Syria (1 Kings 15:18) respectively. Presumably this prior plundering is why there were no 'silver, snuffers, bowls, trumpets … vessels of gold, or of silver' in verse 13.

Let's summarise where we've got to. In Judah the situation is better than in Israel because of the house and the house. God has preserved the Davidic line, and the Temple in their midst continues to bring blessing, not least through the actions of the faithful priest Jehoiada and quick-thinking Auntie Jehosheba. Yet by the end of these chapters, despite some attempts at repairs, the Temple is in decline and robbed of even more of its treasures. Indeed, it will be ransacked again and again until ultimately it is destroyed at the time of the exile. Without the presence of God in their midst, Judah will fare little better than Israel. Will he again dwell in his Temple?

For the new covenant believer there is hope, because of the house and the house! Jesus is the King in the Davidic line whose throne will last forever; God has kept his promises. But he is also the Temple, the presence of God among us, from whom God's gracious, holy rule is extended. When modern-day Athaliahs set up their earthly kingdoms against his, they will be short-lived. His rule will triumph.

What of Jehoiada? He is undoubtedly a type of Christ, in whom we find the ultimate fulfilment of the roles of prophet (like Elisha), king (like David) and priest (like Jehoiada). But might Jehoiada and his wife Jehosheba also serve as role models for those who, not themselves being the Messiah, want to serve the purposes of God in establishing the rule of his Messiah? We could do worse than copy them.

The beginning of the end
2 Kings 13:1 – 17:5

In this section, the author gives us the histories of several kings of Israel and Judah side by side, flipping back and forth between them (as he did in 1 Kings 14:21 - 16:28). Kings of Israel are dated relative to kings of Judah and vice versa. Sometimes the storylines interact directly (Judah attacks Israel in 14:8–14 and then Israel attacks Judah in 16:5). Clearly the author intends that we compare the two.

Israel		Judah
Jehoahaz (13:1–9)		
Jehoash (13:10–25)		
	four generations from Jehu	Amaziah (14:1–22)
Jeroboam II (14:23–9)		
		Azariah (15:1–7)
Zechariah (15:8–12)		
Shallum (15:13–16)		
Menahem (15:17–22)		
Pekahiah (15:23–6)		
Pekah (15:27–31)		
		Jotham (15:32–8)
		Ahaz (16:1–20)
Hoshea (17:1–6)		

We are going to trace the Israel story first. Then we will turn to the story of Judah, mindful of the author's intended comparison.

Dig deeper exercise
Use the AUTHOR'S PURPOSE TOOL. Create some Kings of Israel Top Trumps cards (we've given you the thirteen names above) and consider how well they 'score' on various criteria – e.g., length of reign, evilness rating, grim death rating. What overall patterns do you spot?

The Israel story

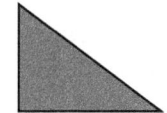

Figure 13 **Israel's decline**

The basic shape of the narrative is decline (see Figure 13). The author's summaries of the kings, which generally top and tail each account, give us several metrics by which we can assess them.

Ever since the kingdom divided after Solomon, Israel's kings have done badly. Reigns are often short – Zimri came bottom of the table at seven days (1 Kings 16:15), but is followed closely by Shallum (one month, 2 Kings 15:13) and Zechariah (six months, 2 Kings 15:8). Almost invariably, they 'did what was evil in the sight of the LORD' (REPETITION TOOL, 2 Kings 13:2, 11; 14:24; 15:9, 18, 24, 28) and 'did not depart from' or 'followed the sins of Jeroboam the son of Nebat, which he made Israel to sin' (REPETITION TOOL, 2 Kings 13:2, 11; 14:24; 15:9, 18, 24, 28). Often they are deposed violently, and references to a proper burial are rare.

The downward slope reaches rock bottom in 17:6, when 'the king of Assyria captured Samaria, and he carried the Israelites away to Assyria'. God had threatened exile as the punishment for breaking his covenant (Leviticus 26:34–9; Deuteronomy 28:63–8), and now it comes to pass.

Having got the basic picture, we are ready to nuance it, and we discover wonderful interventions of God's grace. The first comes in 13:4–5, when 'Jehoahaz sought the favour of the LORD, and the

The downward spiral

Lord listened to him … Therefore the Lord gave Israel a saviour.' God is always ready to show mercy, even to an evil king and a wayward people.

Next, in 13:14–25, J(eh)oash (not to be confused with his namesake in Judah) comes to Elisha's deathbed in desperation, crying something about 'the chariots of Israel and its horsemen'. Is this a rare acknowledgement that the prophetic word has been the hope of Israel, and a realisation that if Elisha dies they will lose the one attended by spiritual armies (CONTEXT TOOL, 6:17)? Or is it simply a reference to Israel's decimation in a recent battle (2 Kings 13:7)? The sophistication of the biblical authors inclines us to think that such ambiguities are deliberate. Either way, God is again gracious, and invites Joash to fire an arrow as a sign of deliverance from the Syrians. We discover subsequently that God is offering multiple victories – one for every arrow that Joash strikes into the ground. Regrettably, in his half-heartedness, he strikes only three times (verse 18) and so wins three battles (verse 25). Had he been faithful, he could have won more. Had the Lord not been merciful, he would have won none.

A little aside: the LINKING WORDS TOOL teaches us to pay particular attention to 'becauses' and 'therefores', and in 13:23 we discover that 'the Lord was gracious to them and had compassion on them, and he turned towards them, *because* of his covenant with Abraham, Isaac, and Jacob' (emphasis added). If someone asked you what might be the biggest reason for hope in 1 – 2 Kings, you would probably (and correctly) cite God's promise to David in 2 Samuel 7, which applies only in Judah. It comes as a bit of a surprise, then, to be reminded here of the prior promise that applies to all twelve tribes of Israel. As the northern kingdom goes off into exile, no more will be heard of them in Israel's history (although there are hopeful mentions in the prophets[1]), until Jesus meets a woman at a well who is from Samaria and he offers forgiveness and restored relationship with God once more (John 4:1–42).

---

1 For example, Ezekiel 37:15–28; Hosea 1:10–11; 2:14–23; Amos 9:11–15.

There's one more display of God's grace during the reign of Jeroboam II:

> The LORD saw that the affliction of Israel was very bitter, for there was none left, bond or free, and there was none to help Israel. But the LORD had not said that he would blot out the name of Israel from under heaven, so he saved them by the hand of Jeroboam the son of Joash.
> (2 Kings 14:26–7)

Yes, the prophet who speaks this oracle is the same Jonah (verse 25) who was famously swallowed by a big fish, but please avoid this red herring (pun absolutely intended).

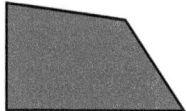

Figure 14 **Taking off the brakes**

God is repeatedly gracious. But notice that his interventions are confined to the first four generations of kings in the line of Jehu, in consequence of a promise made in 2 Kings 10:30. By 15:12, God's obligations to that dynasty have ceased, and we read of no further acts of deliverance. The decline of Israel accelerates rapidly (see Figure 14). It is as if the brakes have been taken off. God no longer holds them back from the precipice. Nothing can stop them from disaster now. The fact that the last king of Israel (Hoshea) was not quite as evil as his predecessors (17:2) is a case of 'too little, too late' – a motif we will see again in the case of Josiah, king of Judah.

The Judah story

Why are we told of Israel and Judah side by side? We see the spiral into doom of Israel and then concurrently we see the same

The downward spiral

mistakes being made in Judah. Like being in Czechoslovakia in 1939 as you watch your government being bullied into giving up the Sudetenland, and then looking over the border at what has happened to Austria with the Anschluss.

But having learnt from the Israel story that God's grace can hold back sin and judgement, we feel more optimistic about Judah. The author reminded us in chapter 11 that Judah had the benefit of two significant means of grace – the house (David's line) and the house (the Temple). It is on those that our hopes are pinned. How do they fare?

Let's consider first the kings of Judah. Worryingly, the first three each have an Achilles heel and the fourth is an absolute rotter. The overall story is one of decline, albeit shallower than the decline of Israel (see Figure 15):

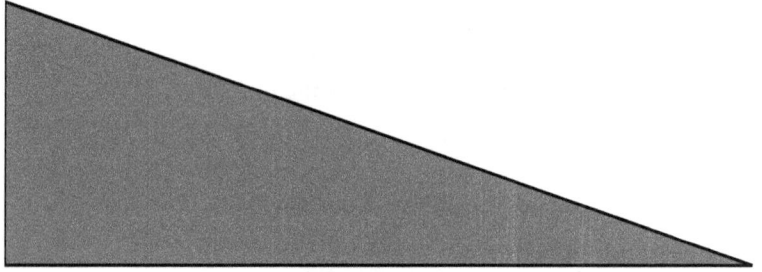

Figure 15 **Judah's decline**

Amaziah 'did what was right in the eyes of the LORD, yet not like David his father' (14:3). He leaves some idolatry unchecked, but he is right not to kill the children of those who assassinated his dad, 'according to what is written in the Book of the Law of Moses' (verse 6).[2] One might say that he got a pass at grade A–C, even if

---

[2] 2 Kings 14:6 and Deuteronomy 24:16 (which it cites) may cause confusion because elsewhere in Scripture, and especially in 1 – 2 Kings, we see judgement falling on a villain's children with God's approval (e.g., Jehu and the sons of Ahab). There is no problem with the idea of corporate responsibility or intergenerational punishment per se. But human beings are fallible, and God's law places limits on the judicial authority of the state in various ways. For instance, coveting is wrong, but not punishable by human courts because thought-crimes are beyond human scrutiny. A descendant may in God's eyes be guilty for the sin of his father (think of

not an A*. How tragic, then, that he decides to wage war against Israel, driven entirely by pride (14:10). This leads to his downfall.

Azariah (aka Uzziah) 'did what was right in the eyes of the LORD' (15:3). But the LORD touched him with leprosy (15:5), meaning of course that he was unclean and would not have been able to enter the Temple. As with Amaziah, he leaves the high places intact.

Jotham 'did what was right in the eyes of the LORD' (15:34), but again turned a blind eye to idolatry.

Ahaz is the rotter. He 'did not do what was right in the eyes of the LORD his God ... but he walked in the ways of the kings of Israel' (16:2–3). This isn't good news for those who are following the Israel story and are hoping for a different trajectory in Judah. Alongside terrible abominations in the Temple, on which more below, we read that he even burnt his own son as an offering to a Canaanite idol.

The story of the Temple is no more encouraging. If we plot the key data points on a longer timescale, we again see unmistakable decline:

> David was promised it ☺☺☺
> Solomon built it ☺☺☺
> Rehoboam gave away some of its treasure to Shishak ☹
> Asa gave away some of its treasure to Ben-hadad ☹
> Joash gave away some of its treasure to Hazael ☹
> Ahaz now builds a replica Assyrian altar in front of it, moves the proper altar round to the side, invites a pagan king to offer his own sacrifices on it and dismantles other parts (16:8–18) ☹☹☹

Paul's explanation, in Romans 5, of the effect of Adam's sin on all humanity), but this is not punishable by human courts. The law in Deuteronomy is designed to limit the scope of human authority to meting out justice on individuals, unless there is a specific command from God to act differently in a particular case.

Compare and contrast

The theological lesson has been immortalised in the words of the English Reformer John Bradford, who, seeing a criminal being led to his execution, said, 'There but for the grace of God go I.' The Jehu line of Israel is kept by God's grace. After that promise runs out, they spiral down the drain. For those in Judah, the references to David and the Temple all the way through remind us of God's promises, but God's patience is being tested to the limit there too.

Tucked away in 13:20–21, however, there is a wonderful note of hope for the first readers of 1 – 2 Kings, in exile in Babylon. 'If only Elisha were still here,' they might have thought, 'for he offered salvation in the face of coming judgement, but now judgement has come and it's too late.' Perhaps not. Even after his own death, the saviour figure has enduring power to save from death.

It's a remarkable story. A funeral is interrupted by a marauding band of Moabites, and before the mourners even have time to dig a fresh grave, the pallbearers are eager to flee from the invaders and hurl the body into whatever existing tomb happens to be available – and it's Elisha's. Whereupon the corpse makes contact with Elisha's bones and is resurrected!

Later Scripture does not develop a theology of relic-collecting from this (the medieval church got that very wrong, and we commend Calvin's hilarious exposé of the practice to anyone who hasn't read it[3]), but it develops the expectation of resurrection through the prophetic word.

The language of 13:21 is remarkably similar to Ezekiel 37:10. Iain Provan notes that the body is 'thrown' into Elisha's tomb in

---

3 John Calvin, 'Treatise on Relics' (1543), available for free online, e.g., at www.ccel.org/ccel/calvin/treatise_relics.v.html (accessed 31 July 2024). Calvin catalogues the various artefacts, supposedly dating back to the time of Jesus, being venerated in sixteenth-century Europe. Our favourite is the finger with which John the Baptist pointed to Jesus as the Lamb of God: 'There is one at Besançon in the Church of St John the Great, a second at Toulouse, a third at Lyons, a fourth at Florence, and a fifth at St Jean des Aventures, near Maçon. Now I request my readers to examine this subject, and to judge for themselves whether they can believe, that whilst St John's finger, which, according to their own tradition, is the only remainder of his body, is at Florence, five other fingers can be found in sundry other places, or, in short, that six are one, and one is six.'

verse 21 in the same way as God 'throws' Israel into exile in 17:23 (same word in Hebrew).[4] So the hope of resurrection is connected to a hope of return from exile, further strengthening the Ezekiel 37 connection.

When we move from old covenant to new covenant, we need to bear in mind elements of both continuity and discontinuity.

In a gloomy passage such as this, the discontinuity offers great comfort. It was God's grace that slowed the decline of Israel and Judah, but we have more grace; grace sufficient to keep us from falling altogether (Jude 24). Christ was the perfect King, for whom it's an understatement to say that he 'did what was right in the eyes of the LORD'. He went into a heavenly and more perfect temple, to offer himself as a sacrifice for our sin (Hebrews 8 – 10). And through his word the spiritually (and physically) dead are raised to life (John 5:24–9). We are safe with him.

But the continuity is important too. Frequently the apostles warn us not to make the mistakes of previous generations. If we fall away, we will be in desperate trouble just as they were (e.g., Hebrews 3 – 4; 1 Corinthians 10:1–13). Christ will keep us from ruin, but 'we must not put Christ to the test' (1 Corinthians 10:9).

---

4 Iain W. Provan, *1 & 2 Kings* (Grand Rapids: Baker Books, 1995), p. 230.

The fall of Israel
2 Kings 17:6–41

We have mentioned before the benefit of travelling at different 'speeds' through the narrative, depending on what is happening. After taking four chapters covering 13 kings and almost a century's worth of events in one go, we are now slowing right down and looking at a few paragraphs.

> **Dig deeper exercise**
> Mostly 1 – 2 Kings is historical narrative; it simply tells us what happened, in order.
> Use the GENRE TOOL. What shift takes place from verse 7 onwards? Why do you think the author has paused the story for this theological reflection?

The section divides straightforwardly in two, though the arrangement of ideas within each half is more complex:

> verses 6–23 Reasons for the exile of the Israelites from Samaria.
> verses 24–41 Account of the subsequent settlers in Samaria.

Reasons for the exile of the Israelites (2 Kings 17:6–23)

There is a straightforward point to these verses: Israel's sin was terrible and God's judgement against them was deserved. These are two sides of the same coin. Only when we see the horror of evil do we recognise that God is right to be angry. Without a grasp of the 'sinfulness of sin' (as the Puritan Ralph Venning called it), people might think God's judgement harsh or unreasonable. So this is a passage that is worth dwelling upon, even if doing so is not a very pleasant experience.

Starting with the LINKING WORDS TOOL, we read in verse 7 that 'this' (the carrying off of the Israelites to Assyria) 'occurred *because* …', and then in verse 23 we read, '*So* Israel was exiled from their own land to Assyria until this day.' Between these bookends comes the reason for the exile. One fruitful way of approaching it is to identify the main categories in which sin is described throughout the passage, and then meditate on each one in turn:

1 Misplaced fear. They 'feared other gods' (verse 7), whereas they ought to have feared the LORD (compare verse 28).
2 Idolatry. There were high places and Asherah poles everywhere (verses 9–12). They 'went after false idols and became false' (verse 15). There were golden calves and worship of Asherah and Baal (verse 16).
3 Doing evil. 'They burned their sons and their daughters as offerings and used divination and omens and sold themselves to do evil in the sight of the LORD' (verse 17).
4 Refusing to listen. There was rejection of the law of Moses (verse 12) and of the prophets who warned them they were departing from the law of Moses (see the progression from verse 12 to verse 13 to verse 14).
5 Rejecting God's saving grace. God had brought them out of Egypt to belong to him (verse 7), but they reverted to the ways of the other nations.

God's anger is provoked (verses 11, 17) by these things. The Israelites do them and 'therefore' (LINKING WORDS TOOL, verse 18) he is angry. References to him casting them out of his sight (REPETITION TOOL, verses 18, 20, 23) are interleaved with descriptions of their sin. Thus we see that God's anger is not a predisposition, but rather a *just response* to evil, after repeated gracious warnings. It is righteous, appropriate anger.

The author then gives us two postscripts. First, we are told tragically that Judah is also beginning to go the way of Israel (verse 19). Given that the first readers of 1 - 2 Kings were themselves exiles from Judah, this would be a particularly poignant point to have slipped in here. Second, there is a focus on King Jeroboam I (verses 21-2), the first evil king of Israel to whom subsequent villains have been so often compared. This reminds us that a wicked king will always lead the people astray. Our only hope is in a godly king.

Account of the subsequent settlers in Samaria (2 Kings 17:24–41)

This second section describes the fate of those who settle in the region around Samaria after the northern tribes of Israel have been kicked out. Most of the third-person pronouns ('them', 'they') refer to these non-Israelites, with the exception of a few verses (verses 35-9), which are about 'the children of Jacob ... called Israel'. It seems that these Israel verses are inserted into the section predominantly about the new settlers to cause us to compare the two. There are several parallels:

- Like Israel, they are taught how to fear the LORD but then they fail to fear the LORD (verse 28; compare with verse 36 addressed to Israel).
- Like Israel, they sacrifice at high places (verse 32).
- As Israel 'followed the nations that were around them' (verse 15), these people revert to 'the manner of the nations from among whom they had been carried away' (verse 33; see also verse 40).
- As Israel burned their sons and daughters (verse 17), so these people burn their children (verse 31).

Clearly, the point is that the new tenants in the land fare similarly to Israel. But what are we to learn from this? It seems odd that God should be indignant that these people did not fear him (sending lions, verse 25), or that they did pagan things and followed pagan gods. After all, they were pagans! Why expect any more? There seem to be two possible explanations, which are not mutually exclusive.

First, the land itself is holy to the LORD, and cannot stomach ungodly residents. Leviticus 18 provides some helpful theological background. This is not a text directly or indirectly referred to by the author in any way, so we should be careful not to give it too much weight in our interpretation. Yet it is a part of the wider Bible context that helps us think in scriptural categories:

> Do not make yourselves unclean by any of these things, for by all these the nations I am driving out before you have become unclean, and the land became unclean, so that I punished its iniquity, and the land vomited out its inhabitants. But you shall keep my statutes and my rules and do none of these abominations, either the native or the stranger who sojourns among you (for the people of the land, who were before you, did all of these abominations, so that the land became unclean), lest the land vomit you out when you make it unclean, as it vomited out the nation that was before you. (Leviticus 18:24–8)

In other words, the land could not stomach the Canaanites, which is why it vomited them out and Joshua was allowed to conquer it. Later it could not stomach the Israelites, which is why it vomited them out and the Assyrians were allowed to conquer it. But the signs are that it cannot stomach the new settlers either. The search continues for a godly people fit to dwell in a land consecrated to a holy God.

The second possibility is that we are intended to read the whole sorry tale as a failed version of Genesis 12:3: 'in all you all the families of the earth shall be blessed'. It looked promising in 1 Kings 4:34 when 'people of all nations came to hear the wisdom of Solomon, and from all the kings of the earth, who had heard of his wisdom', or in 1 Kings 10 when the Queen of Sheba came to visit and had her breath taken away. But now the 'light to the nations' has become a damp squib. The only faith to which Israel's priest (verse 28) can convert the new tenants of the land is the same compromised faith of Israel. How could they learn any differently from a wayward people?

God was justly angry at Israel for their sin. We are told expressly and very clearly here that this was why they went into exile, and why Judah will go the same way. Those settlers who come afterwards do no better.

God is right to be angry at sin and is right to exclude sinners from the blessings of his presence. This should give us real confidence in God's justice. There's a warning in this for all of us, lest we harden our hearts to his word and turn aside to idols. But, gloriously, for those who trust in the gospel, 'Christ redeemed us from the curse of the law by becoming a curse for us – for it is written, "Cursed is everyone who is hanged on a tree"' (Galatians 3:13).

The king who trusted God
2 Kings 18 – 19

These chapters are (like many others in 1 – 2 Kings!) worthy of the Hollywood blockbuster treatment, but it would be quite a cheap film to cast as there are only three main characters: Hezekiah, king of Judah; the Rabshakeh, emissary of Sennacherib, king of Assyria; and Isaiah, prophet of the LORD (plus some extras playing 'the people who are on the wall', 18:26).

This is also a passage crying out for use of the STRUCTURE TOOL.

> **Dig deeper exercise**
> Imagine you are a screenwriter putting together a screenplay for the film of 2 Kings 18 – 19. Using the STRUCTURE TOOL, how would you divide up the narrative into scenes?

At the beginning, Assyria attacks; at the end, Assyria is defeated; and in the middle there are two cycles of dialogue featuring the three main characters:

18:1–8	Hezekiah (summary)
18:9–18	Assyria attacks
18:19–37	The Rabshakeh
19:1–4	Hezekiah
19:5–7	Isaiah
19:8–13	The Rabshakeh
19:14–19	Hezekiah
19:20–34	Isaiah
19:35–7	Assyria defeated

Hezekiah's reign – at last, a good king (2 Kings 18:1–8)!

Having read a calamitous catalogue of compromised kings over the past few chapters, the author's evaluation of Hezekiah lifts our spirits. Here is a king who 'did what was right in the eyes of the Lord, according to all that David his father had done' (verse 3). What? No qualification? What about the high places to which all the other 'good' kings turned a blind eye? Instead of simply telling us that he 'removed' them, the author wants to celebrate (TONE AND FEEL TOOL) that he 'broke' and 'cut down' and 'broke in pieces' the various objects of false worship (verse 4). The inclusion of the bronze serpent made by Moses in Numbers 21:9 in his iconoclasm serves to show his commitment to eliminating idolatry at every level. An object that once brought salvation has become a snare and must be destroyed. What would Hezekiah have done with the Shroud of Turin? Burned it. What would he have done with the Church of the Holy Sepulchre, now become a place of inter-denominational conflict? Razed it to the ground.

Alongside Hezekiah's root and branch approach to false worship, we read that 'he trusted in the Lord', and in this respect he was unsurpassed (verse 5). We shall see, as we read on, that there is a close connection between his rejection of other gods and his faith in the one true God. Lastly, we are told that 'he rebelled against the king of Assyria and would not serve him' (verse 7). It seems that devotion to the real God of Israel has given him a bit of geopolitical backbone.

The Assyrians are coming (2 Kings 18:9–18)

Yet standing up to the largest empire of the day leads to the inevitable response: aggression. The Assyrians sweep down from the north and destroy the northern kingdom (an event we have already looked at in the previous two chapters). In verse 12 we're given another summary of why God allowed this to happen, along the same lines as the extended theological commentary in chapter 17.

Then the rapacious Assyrians turn their attention to little Judah to the south. At first, Hezekiah's bold stance of rebellion in verse 7 seems to be contradicted by his grovelling in verses 13–16. Indeed, he seems to go further than his predecessors in stripping the Temple of its glory to pay off his aggressors. Remember, though, that verse 7 was a *summary*. His early wobble is airbrushed out of the author's overall evaluation, much as David is remembered without reference to his adultery. We might call this the grace of divine forgetfulness, or, as David put it:

> Blessed is the one whose transgression is forgiven,
>   whose sin is covered.
> Blessed is the man against whom the LORD counts no iniquity.
> (Psalm 32:2)

Cycle 1: Rabshakeh–Hezekiah–Isaiah (2 Kings 18:19 – 19:7)

The **Rabshakeh's** speech is terrifying, but loses some of its force when we realise the extent of his theological naivety. He thinks, for example, that the LORD loved being worshipped at the high places, and so must be very upset that Hezekiah has torn them all down (verse 22). He has got the wrong end of the stick!

And see if you can spot the flaw in the logic of verses 34–5. We might paraphrase it thus: 'I defeated lots of fake gods, so why should I be afraid of the all-powerful Creator of the Universe?' It's like a bunch of overweight blokes from the Hoop and Grapes fancying their chances in the FA Cup final because they are good at FIFA on the PlayStation. Or a visitor to London Zoo confidently climbing into the big cat enclosure, heedless of the warnings, because he never had any problem with his *Lion King* stuffed toy as a toddler.

It is always worth having the REPETITION TOOL at hand. There will not always be important repetition in a passage, but if we never check for it we won't spot it when it is there. In this case, the word 'trust' is used seven times (verses 19, 20, 21 twice, 22, 24, 30).

The Rabshakeh thinks the Lord is just like other gods and that he cannot be trusted. This is the exact inverse of what we read in the author's summary of Hezekiah, who trusted in the one true God and rejected all other gods.

Hezekiah immediately humbles himself before the LORD, goes to the house of the LORD and sends for the LORD's prophet to pray on his behalf, on the basis of the LORD's honour. It is hard to imagine a better response from a godly king in a crisis.

Hezekiah was concerned that the Rabshakeh was 'sent to mock the living God' (verse 4), and the LORD confirms his analysis through the words of **Isaiah**: 'the servants of the king of Assyria *have reviled me*' (verse 6, emphasis added). The Assyrians have picked the wrong fight, and the LORD reassures his faithful king that he need not be afraid.

Cycle 2: Rabshakeh–Hezekiah–Isaiah (2 Kings 19:9–34)

The **Rabshakeh** makes a second appearance, in which he repeats the salient points of his earlier announcement: Hezekiah ought not to trust God (verse 10) because other local or national gods have not fared well against the Assyrian onslaught (verses 11–13). It is essentially the stuffed-toy-*Lion-King* logic again.

Hezekiah once again goes to the house of the LORD and prays. Whereas previously he spoke to Isaiah, an intermediary, of 'the LORD *your* God' (verse 4, emphasis added), he now prays directly to the one he calls 'O LORD *our* God' (verse 19, emphasis added). Hezekiah's little faith at the beginning has grown into a stronger and bolder faith.

Hezekiah repeats his concern that God is being mocked (verse 16), and asks him to intervene so that 'all the kingdoms of the earth may know that you, O LORD, are God alone' (verse 19). This is a wonderfully God-centred prayer. He also sees straight through the Rabshakeh's logic. The only reason Sennacherib beat previous 'gods' is that 'they were not gods' (verse 18).[1] Notice for the fourth

---

1 Our friend Chris Thomson has used this passage and 1 Kings 18:20-39 to argue that the word

2 Kings 18 – 19

time that trust in the true God and rejection of other gods are two sides of the same coin.

Isaiah delivers another word from the LORD, and on this occasion takes thirteen verses to say, basically, 'Sennacherib will lose.' The TONE AND FEEL TOOL encourages us to pause over the details, not primarily to learn more information (though there is some, such as the revelation in verse 25 that the Assyrians' rise to power was God's idea in the first place), but simply to appreciate the gravity of the existing information. Sennacherib, through the Rabshakeh, has taunted God, rather as an unwise heckler takes on a master comedian. Now, through Isaiah, the LORD taunts him back and the laughter is at his expense. Look carefully at how the text achieves this. For example:

> *The use of questions.* Asking, 'Whom have you mocked?' (verse 22) hints at the stupidity of the act before the answer is given. And to ask someone who is delusionally puffed up with his own achievements, 'Did no one tell you that it was actually my doing?' (verse 25) is wonderfully deflating.
>
> *The use of metaphor.* The besieged city Jerusalem is the girl in the playground who points and giggles, or perhaps the attractive young woman who laughs in the face of the man who plucked up the courage to ask her out (verse 21). The proud king Sennacherib is a domesticated animal, led by the nose whichever way God wills (verse 28).

The punchline comes in verse 34: 'I will defend this city to save it, for my own sake' (God will defend his honour when mocked)

---

translated 'god' in the Hebrew Bible does not always refer to a deity perceived as real by the speaker or writer, contrary to what is assumed by many biblical scholars. Accordingly, the fact that biblical writers and characters speak of other 'gods' does not imply a polytheistic worldview. Christopher J. Thomson, 'When is a God Not a God? The Semantics of Biblical Monotheism' (paper presented at the Summer Meeting of the Society for Old Testament Study, Cambridge, 5 September 2023). Chris is currently preparing this paper for academic publication.

'and for the sake of my servant David' (God has not forgotten his 2 Samuel 7 promise).

The 'battle' of Jerusalem (2 Kings 19:35–7)

The destruction of the Assyrian army is total and unusually personal. Previously, God has used deception (2 Kings 3:22–3; 7:6–7) or human agency (2 Kings 13:25), but here the angel of the LORD shows up to execute judgement himself (verse 35). The city is saved! Sennacherib retreats to his imperial city of Nineveh with his tail between his legs (verse 36), and then, in a final ironic twist, is killed by his owns sons while worshipping a false god (verse 37).

In 691 BC, the Assyrians inscribed highlights of their military campaign against Israel, in cuneiform, on what has become known as the Taylor Prism, now on display in the British Museum. There Sennacherib boasts of having captured forty-six of Judah's fortified cities, and describes how he 'shut up' Hezekiah in besieged Jerusalem 'like a bird in a cage'.[2] Elsewhere in the British Museum, a series of carved panels depict the successful Assyrian siege of Lachish, an important defensive post. But nowhere do they commemorate the conquest of Jerusalem for the simple reason that … they lost! It's as if William the Conqueror won the Battle of Hastings but was forced to turn back when he reached London,[3] then ordered that this embarrassing detail be omitted from the Bayeux Tapestry.

Let that be a lesson to you!

Trust in the LORD goes hand in hand with rejection of other gods. That is why Hezekiah can tear down the high places and go straight to the Temple in a time of crisis. It is why he does not need to go anywhere else – no foolish military alliances with

---

2 Alan Millard, 'Sennacherib's Attack on Hezekiah', *Tyndale Bulletin* 36 (1985) pp. 61–77.
3 Thanks to Dr Heath-Whyte of the University of Oxford for providing this analogy.

pagans, no compromise with Canaanite religion, no servitude of Sennacherib himself. The pagan does not understand this, which is why Hezekiah's confidence in God seems like foolishness to the Rabshakeh. Pagans, and semi-pagans, will always distribute their eggs among a number of baskets. Only the true believer trusts God alone.

Trust God with everything and burn all other bridges. Surely that's the moral of the story? But we must not take short cuts to get there. Hezekiah is not everyman, or even every Christian person. He is the king. Thus we must take the by now well-trodden path from a son of David to the ultimate Son of David, the Lord Jesus. He is the one who trusted his Father completely and to the exclusion of all others. Think of Satan's Rabshakeh-like temptation in the wilderness (Luke 4), and his promise that safety could be found in obedience to him. What is Jesus' reply? 'You shall worship the Lord your God, and him only shall you serve.' No mixed portfolios for him. No hedging his bets. Real trust means trust in God alone.

But there is a secondary application to those who follow the faithful king. We do well to identify with the ordinary men and women of Judah, the 'people who are on the wall' (18:26). They hear the enemies' threats but follow their king's command and example (18:36). And so they come to share in the king's salvation.

Turning back the sundial
2 Kings 20

'In those days' (verse 1) is the author's clue that the events of this chapter are not what happened *next* after the LORD's deliverance from the Assyrian siege in chapters 18 – 19. Three features of the text indicate that this is in fact a flashback to what happens a short time before:

- Verse 6 tells us that Hezekiah will reign for a further fifteen years. We know he reigned for twenty-nine years in total (18:2), so we can date his illness to his thirteenth or fourteenth year. The siege occurs in the fourteenth year (18:13).
- Verse 6 also refers to a future deliverance from Assyria, which must surely be the striking down of 185,000 enemy troops by the angel of the LORD that we have already read about (19:35).
- In verse 13, Hezekiah shows the Babylonian emissaries lots of treasures. This presumably predates Hezekiah's handing over of the Temple's treasure to Assyria in 18:15.

So this chapter is out of chronological order. There's nothing wrong with that from a storytelling point of view – well-written television dramas often incorporate flashbacks. But it's helpful to ask what the author is trying to achieve by this narrative device. It seems to us that he is deliberately juxtaposing two scenes about the timing of the coming exile:

    verses 1–11   The blessing of fifteen years added.
    verses 12–21   The judgement that limits security to fifteen years.

Why we don't have a 'SPECULATION TOOL' in the Dig deeper toolkit

One of the skills in reading biblical narrative is to limit your evaluation of characters and their actions to that given by the author. Where he is silent, we should resist the temptation to import our own judgements. We are reminded of G. K. Chesterton's description of Christian idealists falling into two categories: those who base their case 'upon certain things which Christ said' and those who base their case 'upon certain things that Christ forgot to say'.[1]

Hezekiah is a case in point. The author has told us that 'he did what was right in the eyes of the LORD, according to all that David his father had done' and that he 'trusted in the LORD, the God of Israel, so that there was none like him among all the kings of Judah after him, nor among those who were before him' (18:3, 5). In other words, an emphatic thumbs up. But in chapter 20, most commentators we have come across want (without the author's explicit guidance) to give him a thumbs down. Among other things, they say he …

> … was wrong when he 'turned his face to the wall' (verse 2), because this is the same verb used of Ahab's sulking in 1 Kings 21:4. But the expression itself is neutral and merely shows a desire for solitude. Ahab wanted solitude because he coveted Naboth's vineyard and could not have it, which is pathetic. Hezekiah wanted solitude because he was terminally ill, which is surely reasonable?

> … prayed a selfish and self-righteous prayer in verse 3. But Hezekiah's language, including the description of himself as 'righteous', is typical of the lament Psalms of David (e.g., Psalms 17, 26; compare 2 Samuel 22:21–5). When an old covenant believer refers to himself as 'righteous', he does

---

1 G. K. Chesterton, *Heretics* (London: John Lane, 1905), p. 155.

The downward spiral

not mean he is entirely sinless or has earned his own way into God's favour. He just means that he trusts God and has walked in faith before him. You can find something similar in the words of Jesus (e.g., Matthew 7:21–7; 25:31–46) or the Apostle Paul (e.g., Romans 2:5–11; 8:13; Galatians 6:8) or the Apostle Peter (e.g., 1 Peter 3:10–12, quoting Psalm 34).

… was unfaithful when he asked for a sign (verse 8). But asking for a sign isn't always wrong (in Isaiah 7:10–13 Ahaz is rebuked for *not* asking for one). Moreover, given that he suffered from a skin disease (verse 7), the law of Moses would have encouraged him to seek some confirmation from God that he was no longer unclean and was therefore fit to 'go up to the house of the LORD' (verse 8).[2]

… erred when he showed the Babylonian envoys all his treasure (verses 12–13). But the closest biblical parallel is to Solomon displaying his glories to the Queen of Sheba in 1 Kings 10, which we saw was a good thing. Hezekiah may well have been foolish or naïve, but the author gives us no clear grounds for charging him with intentional wrong. The author of Chronicles *does* charge Hezekiah with wrong – see 2 Chronicles 32:25 – and so obviously he was wrong! But we need to allow different Bible authors to bring out different aspects in their storytelling. Here in 2 Kings we know only that Isaiah uses Hezekiah's actions to point to disaster ahead, not that the disaster is caused by his actions.

… cared only about himself, as revealed by his shocking response to God's judgement in verse 19. But even here it's possible to give a more charitable reading. For example, Dale Ralph Davis suggests that Hezekiah might be 'saying Yahweh's word is "good," that is, kind, in that the judgement

---

2 See Leviticus 13 – 14.

has been postponed. So 19b would not reflect Hezekiah's self-centeredness but his gratitude.'[3]

Do not misunderstand us. We are not saying that the purpose of the chapter is to vindicate Hezekiah. Our point is that we are not told enough to evaluate him one way or the other. The author's purpose lies elsewhere: the fate of the king is tied up with the fate of the whole nation, and it is at this level that the theological lessons become clear. We do not think that speculating where the Bible is silent is very fruitful. Far better to focus on the things the author says.

The blessing of fifteen years added (2 Kings 20:1–12)

Isaiah the prophet tells Hezekiah that he is about to die. This alarms us as readers even as it alarms him, for he is a faithful king who trusts God. We have seen already (CONTEXT TOOL) that under the leadership of wicked kings, Israel went into a spiral of decline, culminating in her exile. The kings of Judah had begun to go the same way. Here is a good king, and we want to hang on to him as long as possible.

Accordingly, God's mercy to Hezekiah is mercy for the whole nation. God addresses him as 'the leader of my people' (verse 5), and his restoration to health is tied to deliverance of the city (verse 6). Two mentions of David (verses 5, 6) remind us for the umpteenth time that God is keeping his promise made in 2 Samuel 7.

Notice that God's answer makes explicit the time period. He could say, 'You'll get better from your illness,' but instead he says, 'You'll get better and stay well for fifteen more years.' The extraordinary sign that Hezekiah is given (which requires either the bending of light throughout Judah or a temporary rearrangement of the entire solar system) is also all about time. In an age before quartz watches and pendulum clocks, the length of shadows was

---

[3] Dale Ralph Davis, *2 Kings: The Power and the Fury* (Fearn: Christian Focus, 2005), p. 298.

the primary means of reckoning the hour of the day (e.g., Jeremiah 6:4). The 'steps of Ahaz' function like a sundial. A little patience will suffice to see the shadow go forward, but a divine miracle is required to turn the clock back. The God who rules time chooses to extend the days of Hezekiah and the nation. What a blessing.

> **Dig deeper exercise**
> Time to get out the COPYCAT TOOL. Should ordinary Christians seek to imitate what Hezekiah does in this story, and if not, why not?

The judgement that limits security to fifteen years (2 Kings 20:12–21)

Isaiah the prophet tells Hezekiah that his naïve act of hospitality to strangers from 'a far country, from Babylon' (verse 14) was akin to showing some burglars where you keep your jewellery, how to turn off the alarm system and where to find the spare key under the mat. 'The days are coming,' says the LORD – note another time reference – 'when all ... shall be carried to Babylon. Nothing shall be left' (verse 17).

Worse still, and especially chillingly for those mindful that the hope for Judah lies in God's promise of a preserved Davidic dynasty (and the author has just jogged our memory about this), some of the king's own sons shall be carried away and will be *eunuchs* (verse 18) – we do not need to spell out why this might be problematic for their ongoing genealogy. We've cautioned against reading verse 19 primarily to get inside Hezekiah's head. The more obvious point is that the fifteen years of peace for the nation will be *only* fifteen years. There will be peace and security in his days, but not afterwards. The God who rules time chooses to limit the days of Hezekiah and the nation. Judgement will come.

The first readers of 1 - 2 Kings in exile in Babylon needed to know that Judah escaped the Assyrians because the LORD was more powerful than Sennacherib (chapters 18 - 19). And they also needed to know that Judah did not lose to the Babylonians because

Nebuchadnezzar was more powerful than the Lord. Whether battles are lost or won, and particularly the *timing* of the demise of a nation or a king, lies in the hands of the God who controls time. In his mercy he extends time, giving opportunity for a nation to seek him in repentance. In his justice he limits time, bringing an eventual end to sin and wickedness.

One of the key principles in applying the Old Testament to Christian believers is that God is the same. And so the key lesson of this chapter carries straight over to us today – God is still the Lord of Time.

In his mercy he extends time, giving opportunity for people to seek him in repentance. He has delayed final judgement because he 'is patient towards you, not wishing that any should perish, but that all should reach repentance' (2 Peter 3:9).

In his justice he limits time, bringing an eventual end to sin and wickedness: 'he has fixed a day on which he will judge the world in righteousness by a man whom he has appointed; and of this he has given assurance to all by raising him from the dead' (Acts 17:31).

The New Testament urges us to make the most of the time we have. It is limited.

The beginning of the end (Part 2): too little, too late

2 Kings 21:1 – 23:30

One of the more amusing recent additions to the Oxford English Dictionary is for 'Godwin's Law': 'The theory that as an online discussion progresses, it becomes inevitable that someone or something will eventually be compared to Adolf Hitler or the Nazis, regardless of the original topic.'

When evaluating someone's character, we often make comparisons with others. The archetypal villain is Hitler or Stalin or Genghis Khan. The archetypal saint is Mother Teresa or Nelson Mandela.

This section does the same thing. But in the world of 1 – 2 Kings, the archetypal villains are Ahab (the Baal-worshipping, Naboth-murdering, Elijah-opposing king of Israel) and his predecessor Jeroboam I, at whose door was laid the blame for the ultimate exile of the northern kingdom (see 17:21–3). The archetypal saints are David and Hezekiah, the best of the kings of Judah.

Manasseh and Amon (2 Kings 21)

The headline is that Manasseh and his son Amon are truly evil kings, whose heinous crimes finally provoke God to send Judah into exile. Manasseh is nothing like his father Hezekiah and a lot like Jeroboam I and Ahab.

In fact, the CONTEXT TOOL reveals that he is the *opposite* of Hezekiah, because he systematically reverses his father's campaign against idolatry. Where Hezekiah removed the high places (18:4), he rebuilds them (21:3); where Hezekiah cut down Asherah poles (18:4), he erects them (21:3).

In fact, he does exactly 'as Ahab king of Israel had done' (21:3). With the QUOTATION/ALLUSION TOOL in hand, we discern an echo of the oft-repeated description of 'Jeroboam son of Nebat' who *'made Israel to sin'* (1 Kings 16:26; 21:22; 22:52; 2 Kings 3:3; 10:29; 13:2, 11; 14:24; 15:9, 18, 24, 28; 17:21, emphasis added) when we read that Manasseh *'made Judah [also] to sin'* (21:11, 16, emphasis added). In addition, 21:6 lists some horrific crimes that closely parallel those of the northern kingdom for which they were sent into exile (see Table 17):

'And they burned their sons and their daughters as offerings and used divination and omens and sold themselves to do evil in the sight of the LORD, provoking him to anger.' (2 Kings 17:17)	'And he burned his son as an offering and used fortune-telling and omens and dealt with mediums and with necromancers. He did much evil in the sight of the LORD, provoking him to anger.' (2 Kings 21:6)

Table 17 **Manasseh's sins parallel those of Israel**

These are damning comparisons, but actually Manasseh is even worse than those who went before because he brings idolatry into the Temple itself (verses 4–5, 7). The author emphasises the shock of this sin by reminding us twice that this was the place 'of which the LORD had said … "I will put my name"' (verses 4, 7). What is more, Manasseh has the invidious distinction of doing more evil than the nations whom God drove out of the land before the people of Israel (verses 9, 11). He is the only monarch from either Israel or Judah whose record in the 'Book of the Chronicles of the Kings' mentions his sin (verse 17).

Even before the LORD pronounces his sentence, we can guess where this is going. We know the precedent. The Amorites were evicted from the land because they were evil. The northern kingdom was evicted from the land because it was evil. So exile for Judah is now also inevitable.

The author highlights the connection between Manasseh's crimes and the LORD's punishment in two main ways. First, the REPETITION TOOL/VOCABULARY TOOL reveals a play on words: Manasseh 'did evil' (i.e., he sinned, verses 2, 6, 11), leading the people to do evil (i.e., they sinned, verses 9, 15, 16) so that the LORD says he is 'bringing upon Jerusalem and Judah ... evil' (verse 12, see literal translation in ESV footnote).

Second, the LINKING WORDS TOOL shows us that the punishment is sandwiched between a 'therefore' (verse 12) and a 'because' (verse 15), connecting it closely to the crime (exactly the same device was used in 17:7, 23).

Having understood that the punishment is fully deserved, we are invited to dwell briefly on its terrifying nature. Three images stick in our minds:

- The tingling ears of those who hear of the fall of Jerusalem (verse 12) – a colourful Hebrew idiom that means what it says.[1]
- The holding up of the measuring line of Samaria and plumb line of Ahab (verse 13) – and if what happened to them sets the standard for just deserts, then it's not looking good.
- The picture of God turning his dish upside down and wiping it out (verse 13) – the cleansing effect of judgement will be total.

Little needs to be said about Amon. He is a chip off the old block (verses 20–21), and he dies ignominiously (verse 24).

Josiah (2 Kings 22:1 – 23:30)

The headline here is that Josiah is a good king who brings godly reforms and leads the nation to repentance. Josiah is nothing like his father Manasseh and a lot like our heroes Hezekiah and David.

---

[1] The same expression is used in 1 Samuel 3:11 and Jeremiah 19:3, both in the context of impending doom.

We know he is like David because the author explicitly tells us in 22:2. The CONTEXT TOOL shows us that he is nothing like Manasseh (and a lot like Hezekiah), because he systematically roots out his father's idolatry. He burns pagan vessels (23:4), deposes false priests (23:5), reduces Asherah poles to ash and 'cast the dust of it upon the graves of the common people' (23:6), 'broke down the houses of the male cult prostitutes' (23:7), 'defiled the high places' (23:8), including Topheth 'that no one might burn his son or his daughter as an offering to Molech' (23:10), removes sun worship objects (23:11), smashes false altars and high places associated with previous kings of Judah, undoing idolatry that goes back to Solomon (23:12-13).

Josiah's reforms extend even into the former northern kingdom of Israel, where he finally deals with the golden calf altar set up by Jeroboam at Bethel. It seems he is at first unaware of the significance of his actions, being told subsequently of the word of the Lord from a man of God that predicted the reign of a man called Josiah who would burn bones on this very altar (23:17; see 1 Kings 13:1-2). Once again, an amazing reminder that God's word always comes to pass, even through the unknowing acts of someone centuries later.

As if all this were not enough, he reinstates the Passover (23:21), gets rid of idols at every level of society and seeks to 'establish the words of the law' (23:24) - i.e., he wants the people of Judah once again to live according to what God says. In summary, says the author:

> Before him there was no king like him, who turned to the Lord with all his heart and with all his soul and with all his might, according to all the Law of Moses, nor did any like him arise after him.
> (2 Kings 23:25)

In picking out choice details from Josiah's reign, however, we have actually jumped the gun. As a discerning reader, you ought to have been concerned with our skipping over chapter 22 - beware sermons

The downward spiral

and Bible studies that pick and choose! In fact, the STRUCTURE TOOL will show us that chapter 22 is rather crucial to the whole:

22:1–2	Opening summary.
22:3–20	Law found by Hilkiah and consequences of breaking it prophesied by Huldah.
23:1–23	Josiah's reforms (bracketed by references to the Book of the Covenant, verses 2, 21).
23:24–7	Reminder of the law being found (Hilkiah) and consequences of breaking it (Huldah).
23:28–30	Closing summary.

The effects of the Hilkiah–Huldah brackets are twofold. First, they emphasise that the impetus for Josiah's reforms is the rediscovery of God's law. In this respect, the story of Josiah departing from the wicked ways of his father Manasseh thanks to being given a copy of the law by a faithful priest (Hilkiah) closely parallels the previous story of Joash departing from the wicked ways of his grandmother Athaliah thanks to being given a copy of the law by the faithful priest Jehoiada (2 Kings 11 – 12).

It's amazing to think that Israel has drifted so far from its spiritual moorings that they have forgotten that part of the Bible even *exists*. And then Hilkiah finds some dusty manuscript in the back of a storeroom in the Temple. It reminds us of the astonishing story of the nineteenth-century scholar Tischendorf visiting St Catherine's monastery on the Sinai Peninsula, where he discovered, in an old basket (among other baskets that contained scraps of parchment that the monks were using as kindling to start fires!), what turned out to be the oldest surviving copy of the entire New Testament in Greek.[2] 'Could this be important, anybody?'

Nowadays, it's not that we've lost the Bible. You can buy a copy in any bookshop. But sometimes the Church has forgotten what it says. When the word of God is rediscovered, there is hope.

---

2 Although the story may have grown somewhat in the telling; see the excellent history of subsequent events in Janet Soskice, *Sisters of Sinai: How Two Lady Adventurers Found the Hidden Gospels* (London: Vintage, 2010).

Second, the brackets tell us that the consequences of God's covenant having been broken will be defeat and exile:

> Thus says the LORD, Behold, I will bring disaster upon this place and upon its inhabitants, all the words of the book that the king of Judah has read. Because they have forsaken me and have made offerings to other gods, that they might provoke me to anger with all the work of their hands, therefore my wrath will be kindled against this place, and it will not be quenched.
> (2 Kings 22:16–17)

> Still the LORD did not turn from the burning of his great wrath, by which his anger was kindled against Judah, because of all the provocations with which Manasseh had provoked him. And the LORD said, 'I will remove Judah also out of my sight, as I have removed Israel, and I will cast off this city that I have chosen, Jerusalem, and the house of which I said, My name shall be there.'
> (2 Kings 23:26–7)

We need to think carefully about the relationship of this prophecy to the reforms that come in between. By structuring it this way, the author emphasises that *we already know that the reforms cannot avert exile*, before they even begin. Does this mean that Josiah is embarking on a foolish mission? Or worse, that he is attempting, like a legalist, to work his own way into God's favour? No. The text gives no hint that Josiah is doing anything wrong. On the contrary, he is praised repeatedly.

Josiah's efforts at reform and his leading of the people to repentance is wholly right. But repentance by itself cannot atone for past wrongs. This is the big theological lesson of the chapter.

Dig deeper exercise

Using the CONTEXT TOOL, compare the fall of Israel in 2 Kings 13 – 17 with the fall of Judah here. What is the same? What is different?

Too little, too late

If we've got so close to the details that we've missed the wood for the trees, it may be helpful to take a step back and summarise:

1 Manasseh and Amon – really bad.
2 Josiah – really good.
3 But the really good cannot cancel out the really bad.

Once a nation has broken God's law, repentance is not enough. We also need atonement and forgiveness. Some of that was provided for in the law itself, of course, and the provision of a hotline by which prayers for mercy might reach heaven was one of the key blessings of the Temple (see 1 Kings 8). But really serious evil requires really serious atonement, which has not yet come.

> Not the labours of my hands
> Can fulfill thy law's demands
> Could my zeal no respite know
> Could my tears forever flow
> All for sin could not atone
> Thou must save, and thou alone.[3]

A lazy attempt to apply 2 Kings says simply, 'Josiah failed; Jesus succeeded.' But we ought not to neglect the continuities between them (or, in different terminology, the extent to which Josiah is a 'type' of Jesus). Josiah was the anointed king of God's people, as is Jesus. Josiah rooted out idolatry, particularly in the Temple, as did Jesus (e.g., Luke 19:45–6). Josiah was concerned to live according to God's law, as was Jesus.

But Josiah could not atone for sin. And neither could the law that he rightly sought to live by. Yet wonderfully, in the Lord Jesus:

---

3 Augustus Montague Toplady (1740–78) 'Rock of Ages'.

2 Kings 21:1 – 23:30

God has done what the law, weakened by the flesh, could not do. By sending his own Son in the likeness of sinful flesh and for sin, he condemned sin in the flesh, in order that the righteous requirement of the law might be fulfilled in us, who walk not according to the flesh but according to the Spirit. (Romans 8:3–4)

The fall of Judah
2 Kings 23:31 – 25:26

The end of 1 – 2 Kings is a story of persistent decline, defeat, deportations. We will explore some of the sub-themes in a moment, but it is instructive to notice that many features of the narrative come in pairs (see Table 18).

Jehoahaz reigned for only three months (23:31)	Jehoiachin reigned for only three months (24:8)
Jehoahaz imprisoned by Pharoah Neco (23:33)	Jehoiachin imprisoned by Nebuchadnezzar (24:12)
Pharaoh Neco installed Eliakim as king, and changed his name to Jehoiakim (23:34)	Nebuchadnezzar installed Mattanaiah as king and changed his name to Zedekiah (24:17)
Jehoahaz went to Egypt (23:34)	People fled from the Chaldeans to Egypt (25:26)
Jehoiakim reigned for eleven years (23:36) then foolishly rebelled (24:1)	Zedekiah reigned for eleven years (24:18) then foolishly rebelled (24:20)
Nebuchadnezzar besieged Jerusalem (24:10)	Nebuchadnezzar besieged Jerusalem (25:1)
Temple ransacked for gold (24:13)	Temple ransacked for bronze (25:13–17)
Deportation of the men of valour (24:14)	Deportation of the ordinary residents (25:11)

Table 18 **Spot the difference**

The parallels are so strong that they must be deliberate, on the part of both the God who planned history and the inspired author who wrote it up in such a way as to draw our attention to it.

2 Kings 23:31 – 25:26

> **Dig deeper exercise**
> This final passage calls for the most important, multifunctional tool in the toolkit, the AUTHOR'S PURPOSE TOOL. Attention is obviously drawn to the fact that everything is in pairs. But why?

At the very least the repeated pairs indicate that the decline of Judah was not accidental or random. Exact numerical coincidences in length of reigns – three months, eleven years, three months, eleven years – bear the hallmark of God's planning.

Moreover, the fact that the Babylonian invasion comes in several waves also serves to underline the comprehensiveness of the judgement. We are reminded of the metaphor of a dish, wiped out and turned upside down, so that nothing is left (CONTEXT TOOL, 21:13):

- Men of valour are taken (24:14), then everyone else except vine dressers and ploughmen (25:11-12), and then they flee too (25:26) leaving no one at all.
- Gold is stripped out of the Temple (24:13), then bronze is stripped out (25:13-17), leaving nothing at all.

While most of the events in these chapters are grim, some have particular theological significance. The glory of Israel consisted in:

- Her king (and the promise of an eternal Davidic dynasty; see 2 Samuel 7). But now kings' names are changed by foreign overlords, signalling their subjection. And the line of succession is under severe threat, and even *looks like* it might have been wiped out: Jehoahaz dies in exile (23:34) so the crown passes to his brother Jehoiakim, then to his son Jehoiachin (24:6), who is captured and taken away so that the crown passes to his uncle Zedekiah (24:17) whose sons are murdered before his eyes (25:7). So with no members of the royal family left, a man called Gedaliah is appointed governor (25:22).
- Her salvation from Egypt, remembered many times in 1 – 2 Kings (e.g., 1 Kings 8:9, 16, 21, 51; 2 Kings 17:7, 36), not least in the Passover recently celebrated by Josiah (23:21-3). But

The downward spiral

now they *return* to Egypt (23:34; 25:26). Judgement is salvation reversed.
- Her Temple, the house for God's name, full of splendour and glory, offering a hotline to God, by which his forgiveness could be sought (see 1 Kings 8:27–53). But now it is stripped of its glory and burned to the ground (25:9).

The author twice tells us why all of this has happened (three times, if we include the prophecies of 21:1–15). It is worth focusing in on these verses:

> Surely this came upon Judah at the command of the LORD, to remove them out of his sight, for the sins of Manasseh, according to all that he had done, and also for the innocent blood that he had shed. For he filled Jerusalem with innocent blood, and the LORD would not pardon.
> (2 Kings 24:3–4)

There seem to be two steps here. Punishment comes because of evil. And punishment cannot be averted because of the lack of pardon. Sin without atonement is a terrible thing. 'For because of the anger of the LORD it came to the point in Jerusalem and Judah that he cast them out from his presence' (24:20).

This verse puts exile in, theologically speaking, the most horrific terms. Not only are they being thrown out of the land, but they are also being cast out of God's presence. He cannot stand to be with them any more.

Hope is dead.

Coda
2 Kings 25:27–30

A final twist. Hope is not dead. The royal line has not been snuffed out. Only now do we discover that Jehoiachin, son of Josiah, is alive and well after all, free from prison and dining at the king's table. Perhaps he might have a son? And his son might have another son? And the 2 Samuel promise of an eternal kingdom might be fulfilled, after all?

Unfaithfulness to God's covenant led to devastating judgement. Every blessing was withdrawn. And there came a point when even mercy ran out. But God never breaks his promises. And the promise that a Son of David would always sit on the throne gives a glimmer of hope to the exiles who would have been the first readers of this book. The theme is taken up by some of the prophets in the exilic and post-exilic period:

> And it shall come to pass in that day, declares the Lord of hosts, that I will break his yoke from off your neck, and I will burst your bonds, and foreigners shall no more make a servant of him. But they shall serve the Lord their God and David their king, whom I will raise up for them.
>
> Then fear not, O Jacob my servant, declares the Lord,
>   nor be dismayed, O Israel;
> for behold, I will save you from far away,
>   and your offspring from the land of their captivity.
> Jacob shall return and have quiet and ease,
>   and none shall make him afraid.
> (Jeremiah 30:8–10)

The downward spiral

Rejoice greatly, O daughter of Zion!
　　Shout aloud, O daughter of Jerusalem!
Behold, your king is coming to you;
　　righteous and having salvation is he,
humble and mounted on a donkey,
　　on a colt, the foal of a donkey.
I will cut off the chariot from Ephraim
　　and the war horse from Jerusalem;
and the battle bow shall be cut off,
　　and he shall speak peace to the nations;
his rule shall be from sea to sea,
　　and from the River to the ends of the earth.
As for you also, because of the blood of my covenant with you,
　　I will set your prisoners free from the waterless pit.
Return to your stronghold, O prisoners of hope;
　　today I declare that I will restore to you double.
(Zechariah 9:9–12)

And then, wonderfully, here is how the story continues in Matthew 1:10–16:

Hezekiah [was] the father of Manasseh, and Manasseh the father of Amos, and Amos the father of Josiah, and Josiah the father of Jechoniah and his brothers, at the time of the deportation to Babylon ...

[Is this the end of the line?]

... And after the deportation to Babylon: Jechoniah was the father of Shealtiel, and Shealtiel the father of Zerubbabel, and Zerubbabel the father of Abiud, and Abiud the father of Eliakim, and Eliakim the father of Azor, and Azor the father of Zadok, and Zadok the father of Achim, and Achim the father of Eliud, and Eliud the father of Eleazar, and Eleazar the father of Matthan, and Matthan the father of Jacob, and Jacob

the father of Joseph the husband of Mary, of whom Jesus was born, who is called Christ.
(Matthew 1:10–16)

Praise be to the God and Father of our Lord Jesus Christ. Where sin abounded, grace abounded much more.

Scripture and other copyright acknowledgements

Unless otherwise noted, Scripture quotations are taken from the ESV Bible (The Holy Bible, English Standard Version), copyright © 2001 by Crossway, a publishing ministry of Good News Publishers. Used by permission. All rights reserved.

Scripture quotations marked NIV are taken from The Holy Bible, New International Version (Anglicized edition). Copyright © 1979, 1984, 2011 by Biblica. Used by permission of Hodder & Stoughton Ltd, an Hachette UK company. All rights reserved. 'NIV' is a registered trademark of Biblica. UK trademark number 1448790.

Scripture quotations marked NLT are taken from the *Holy Bible*, New Living Translation, copyright © 1996. Used by permission of Tyndale House Publishers, Inc., Carol Stream, Illinois 60189, USA. All rights reserved.

Extracts from The Book of Common Prayer, the rights in which are vested in the Crown, are reproduced by permission of the Crown's Patentee, Cambridge University Press.

Every effort has been made to seek permission to use copyright material reproduced in this book. The publisher apologizes for those cases where permission might not have been sought and, if notified, will formally seek permission at the earliest opportunity.

CHECK OUT THE WWW.DIGDEEPER.TOOLS WEBSITE FOR VARIOUS FREE RESOURCES

including quirky videos introducing some of the tools (e.g. the one where Andrew makes seven costume changes in seven seconds) and a series of ready-to-go small-group Bible studies on 1 & 2 Kings that you could use in conjunction with this book.

FIND OUT MORE

Dig deeper into the Gospel of Mark in this rejacketed edition of *Dig Deeper into the Gospels* by Andrew Sach and Tim Hiorns

Paperback | 9781789745689
Ebook | 9781789745696

Dig deeper into the book of Exodus in this rejacketed edition of *Dig Even Deeper*, by Andrew Sach and Richard Alldritt

Paperback | 9781789745702
Ebook | 9781789745719

The *Dig Deeper* series
from IVP

More resources from IVP
to help you dig into 1 & 2 Kings

9781783590315

9781844742646

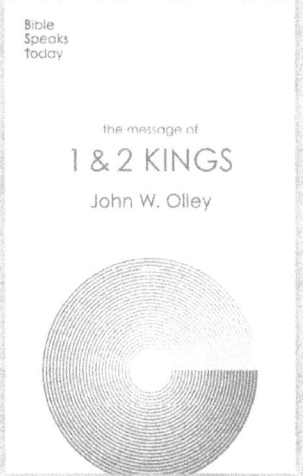

9781789743814

9781783596751